C0-ASZ-917

COOKIES

U-gotten of salve

COOKIES

80 crunchy, nutty, chewy
and chocolatey recipes—
from old-fashioned favorites
to new taste treats

Diane Rozas & Rosalee Harris

A Particular Palate Cookbook
Harmony Books / New York

A Particular Palate Cookbook

Copyright © 1984 by Diane Rozas and Rosalee Harris

All rights reserved. No part of this book may be reproduced or transmitted in any form or by any means, electronic or mechanical, including photocopying, recording, or by any information storage and retrieval system, without permission in writing from the publisher.

Published by Harmony Books, a division of Crown Publishers, Inc., One Park Avenue, New York, New York 10016, and simultaneously in Canada by General Publishing Company Limited

HARMONY, PARTICULAR PALATE, and colophons are trademarks of Crown Publishers, Inc.

Manufactured in the United States of America

Library of Congress Cataloging in Publication Data

Rozas, Diane.
  Cookies.

  1. Cookies. I. Harris, Rosalee. II. Title.
TX772.R69   1984   641.8'654   84-3790
ISBN 0-517-55406-2 (pbk.)

10 9 8 7 6 5 4 3 2 1

First Edition

This book is for Joan Wenzel, who knows a good cookie when she tastes one. (D.R.)

For Jay, whose support and enthusiasm for cookies has yet to wane. (R.H.)

Contents

COOKIES

Introduction

"Cookie" is a wonderful, emotion-filled word used to describe a smallish, sweet, hand-held morsel of magic that comes in myriad shapes, sizes, textures, tastes and designs.

Cookies can be dry and crisp, moist and chewy, crumbly and crunchy. They can envelop the palate in sweet bursts of chocolate, nuts, fruits, liqueurs and essences. They can be filled, topped, iced and colored to entice the eye.

From country to country, in their many traditional forms and flavors, cookies play a major roll in holiday feasting (just try to imagine Christmas without an attractive assortment), as well as everyday eating in others (now try to imagine a lunchbox without a brownie tucked into the corner). It is in our kitchens that cookies take on an ever-greater variety of attributes and homemade charms, for it is in home kitchens that traditional recipes are changed by the whims and wishes of the cook. The recipes then become jealously guarded secrets, usually listed on grease-stained file cards, renamed for their re-creators, i.e., "Aunt Helen's Walnut Wonders" or "Grannie Risë's Butter Spritz."

What really makes one baker's cookies so different from another's? Very little. Since most cookie recipes call for nearly the same ingredients and use the same basic baking methods in their making, the real difference could be as small as a pinch of nutmeg or perhaps more humidity in the air on the day of baking. In other words, most cookie recipes are classic recipes or an interpretation thereof.

As edibles go, cookies tend to have their own innate powers over our taste buds—one is seldom enough—as well as our memories. The smell of a cookie baking can send the mind traveling back on a very personal sojourn to days gone by, to people and places long since past. A cookie can soothe the soul as easily as a kind word. Just as it would be difficult to find a person who didn't like kind words, so would it be difficult to find a person who didn't like cookies. Therefore, a book for baking these special treasures of taste is a must on any kitchen shelf.

Cookie recipes number into the hundreds, and the problem of which to include in this slim volume loomed large. Those types of fancy cookies usually made better by highly trained bakers were not included in order that this labor of love—baking cookies—would not become a labor in itself. Also, many cookie recipes possess different names but have almost identical ingredients, in identical amounts. In these cases, only the best were included and in their best form, which was determined only after several testings and plenty of adjustments. However, a good many of the recipes in this book offer a plethora of wonderful variations which should keep you happily baking delicious and delightful cookies for a long time to come.

Leaf through the beginning chapters of this book and you will encounter a special section devoted to brownies; another section on that all-time American favorite, the chocolate chip cookie; then sections including cookie recipes that are prepared by using the same techniques—dropped, rolled, molded, hand-formed and shaped cookies. Surely your favorites are here. We hope that new favorites will be found within this selection of wonderful cookie recipes.

Ingredients

Besides butter, flour, sugar and flavorings, several other important ingredients go into cookie making, namely, time, money, emotions and anticipation of the results. Wouldn't it be a shame to throw all that away by starting out with less than the finest ingredients available?

A word to the wise: What goes into a cookie is what comes out. When you start with the freshest eggs, the sweetest butter, perfectly crunchy nuts, sun-dried raisins and rich, dark chocolate—you'll bake the best cookies. And that's a fact.

BUTTER Butter provides a delicate, creamy taste and texture that no other fat or shortening can. We strongly suggest that you use only unsalted butter. Salt is called for in the proper amount for each individual recipe. Margarine is not recommended because it produces a different texture; also, drop cookies tend to spread much more while baking and rolled cookie dough becomes far more difficult to handle. Stick with fresh, sweet butter and you'll bake wonderful-tasting, beautiful-looking cookies every batch. Butter freezes very well, too; keep a supply on hand for when the urge to bake cookies hits.

CHOCOLATE The three types of chocolate commonly called for throughout the recipes in this book are unsweetened baking chocolate, semisweet chocolate (chips and individually wrapped 1-ounce squares) and unsweetened Dutch-process cocoa powder. They are not interchangeable within the recipes because they contain different amounts of sugar and cocoa butter. Some books dealing solely with the subject of chocolate cookery offer formulas for substituting one type of chocolate for another; however, an educated guess is not reliable. There is one exception to the rule: Bittersweet chocolate may be used in place of semisweet chocolate, but this is strictly a preference of the palate.

CREAM, SOUR CREAM, CREAM CHEESE AND MILK The key is "fresh." If you have doubts about the age of your dairy products, try another recipe until you can get to the store. When "heavy cream" is called for, choose whipping cream. Buy cream cheese without salt.

EGGS All eggs should be large grade A eggs, as fresh as possible. It's much easier to separate eggs when they are cold, and there's less chance of breaking the yolk into the white. Before adding eggs to any other ingredients, allow them to stand at room temperature for a minimum of 15 minutes.

Egg Yolks. Leftover egg yolks can be stored for 3 to 4 days in the refrigerator. Place a tablespoon of water over the top of the yolk, seal tightly; drain off the water before using.

Egg Whites. Before beating egg whites,

bring them to room temperature. Use a clean, dry glass or stainless-steel or copper bowl free of oil or grease. Avoid using plastic bowls; they are porous and retain grease.

Egg whites can be stored in the freezer almost indefinitely. One simple way of doing so is to place each egg white in a small plastic sandwich bag. To thaw, remove the number of whites you want, and allow them to stand at room temperature for approximately 1 hour.

FLOUR Throughout this book, all-purpose flour is called for in almost every recipe. All-purpose flour is presifted in the refining process and in most cases does not require re-sifting. Always store flour in a cool, dry place and make sure your flour supply is fresh, too. If you don't bake frequently, store flour in an airtight container in the freezer. To measure flour, gently spoon into a dry measure cup and level off with a straight knife or spatula. When measuring sifted flour, first shake the flour through a strainer or sieve onto wax paper, then gently spoon it into the measuring cup and level it off. Never pack the flour into the cup. Whole-wheat flour is much denser than all-purpose flour and should not be substituted.

FRUIT *Dried Fruit.* Dried fruit, yes. Dried out, old, chemically treated fruit, no. The adage "what you put in is what you get out" could not apply more aptly than to baking with dried and candied fruit. Dried fruit adds not only texture and color to cookies but is often the predominant taste. To ensure freshness, buy your dried fruit in a health-food store or specialty shop with a wide variety of raisins, figs, dates, apricots, currants and other fruits.

Candied Fruit. A few recipes, especially for holiday cookies, call for candied fruit. Avoid the small plastic containers of candied fruit that suddenly appear in the grocery stores around Thanksgiving and Christmas; they have been sitting in warehouses all year. Specialty shops carry a fresher, higher-quality selection of candied fruits, both mixed and separate fruits, which are very flavorful. Sources for fine candied fruit can be found in the Mail-Order Guide (see page 119). Do not refrigerate or freeze candied fruit or it will crystallize and become unusable; store it in an airtight glass jar.

NUTS Cookies and nuts are inseparable. Almost every kind of nut on earth is called for throughout this collection of cookie recipes. Nuts add flavor, texture and, often, beauty to cookies. They must, of course, be the freshest available. Sometimes, even though recently purchased, the nuts may not be totally fresh. Nuts should be crunchy, aromatic, sweet tasting and never bitter or rancid smelling. If possible, taste them before buying.

Toasted Nuts. To enhance their flavor, bake unshelled nuts in a 350° F. oven for 10 to 15 minutes, checking several times to make sure the nuts are browning evenly. Shake the pan several times so they don't burn.

Blanched Nuts. Blanching means removing the skins. With some nuts this is very important; with others it is a matter of taste and appearance. Almonds and hazelnuts are almost always blanched before being used in baking. To blanch almonds, submerge them in boiling water for 2 to 5 minutes, then squeeze the nut out of the skin. For hazelnuts (filberts), toast them in a 350° F. oven for 10 to 15 minutes, then rub the skins off with a clean, dry dishcloth.

Ground Nuts. Grind nuts in a food processor or nut grinder just before using. Store nuts in an airtight container in the freezer or the refrigerator to prevent them from turning rancid. This will not spoil their delicate flavor in the least.

OATMEAL There are many varieties of oatmeal, and each one imparts different density and chewiness to cookies. Use oatmeal that takes 3 to 5 minutes to cook. Never use instant oatmeal.

SPICES AND FLAVORINGS Ideally, you should buy all your spices whole and grind them fresh for each recipe, use vanilla from a bean, and not a bottle of extract, and so on. Realistically, there are several suggestions that will help you to get the best flavors into your cookies without losing integrity.

Extracts. Purchase "pure" vanilla and almond extract and only from a reputable manufacturer. Avoid "imitation" extracts at all costs. Take special care to cover the bottles tightly; if they have begun to evaporate, discard them immediately. Measure carefully as some extracts (especially almond) are more potent than you might think.

Spices. Purchase spices at a culinary specialty store (see Mail-Order Guide, page 119) whenever possible. Throw out spices that have lost their zip; they are useless in terms of adding flavor to anything. Always store spices away from heat and light in airtight, opaque containers.

Orange and Lemon Zest. Dehydrated, grated lemon and orange peel are not suitable substitutes for fresh. Zest (only the colored part of the skin, not the bitter white part) should be grated just before using as its delicate flavor dissipates quickly, or store citrus zest in an airtight container in the refrigerator or in a plastic sandwich bag in the freezer. To prepare zest: Grate the zest from 6 lemons or 4 oranges and combine with 3 tablespoons of the fresh juice and 1 cup granulated sugar. It will retain its flavor and aroma for up to 6 months. One tablespoon of this prepared zest is equal to 1 teaspoon freshly grated zest.

Liqueurs. There's nothing like the real thing. When the alcohol evaporates during the cooking process, a delightful depth of flavor is imparted to the cookies.

SWEETENERS Different sugars and sweeteners impart specific flavors to cookies. There are many—granulated sugar being the most common. Other sugars, such as dark and light brown sugar, are used to achieve a special flavor effect and should not be substituted for granulated. Nor should confectioners' sugar (also called X-10 or powdered sugar), as it changes the texture of the dough and melts differently when baked. Liquid sweeteners like molasses, dark and light corn syrup and honey are used to add special flavors as well. Superfine is exactly that—very fine granulated sugar. It is especially nice for dusting cookies after they have been baked.

Crystal sugar and colored sugar are strictly for decorating.

Flavored sugars such as vanilla sugar, cinnamon sugar, lemon or orange sugar are not only sweeteners but flavor enhancers as well. Hand-formed cookies are sometimes rolled in these flavored sugars before or after baking; however, these sugars do not have the intensity or impart the same flavors as do zest or pure extracts. This is not to say that flavored sugars are not an important part of a recipe, but their flavors are a more subtle addition.

Vanilla Sugar. Place a whole vanilla bean inside a container of granulated, confectioners' or superfine granulated sugar. Leave it for 3 or 4 days and the sugar will then be perfumed with vanilla and ready to use. One vanilla bean can flavor many pounds of sugar; refill the container as the vanilla sugar is used up. Store airtight in a cool place.

Orange or Lemon Sugar. Add 1 teaspoon freshly grated zest or 1 tablespoon prepared zest (see page 15) to 1 cup granulated sugar.

Cinnamon Sugar. Mix 1 cup granulated sugar with 2 to 3 tablespoons ground cinnamon. Store in an airtight container until you are ready to use.

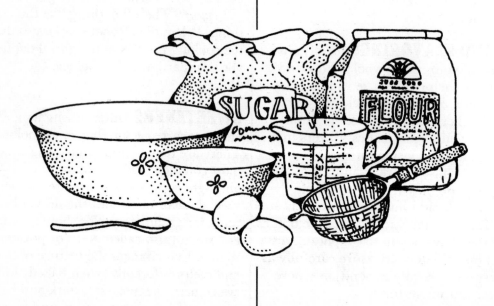

Equipment

The simplest equipment can make the tastiest assortment of cookies. Since the key is—and always will be—the quality of the ingredients, your investment in equipment need not be extravagant. Mixing can be done successfully with just a wooden spoon and almost any bowl (though plastic is not recommended). However, proper measuring tools are essential!

For making fancier, more beautifully shaped cookies, especially those that make delicious edible gifts at holiday time, you may want to start a collection of treasured cookie cutters, tartlet pans, molds or plaques (used for madeleines). This type of equipment will be around for a long time—just look in the antique stores for the proof.

BOWLS A variety of stainless-steel, pottery or enamel-coated mixing bowls of various sizes is important. Small, medium and large bowls are needed at different stages of the cookie-making process. You should have at least one of each size.

CAKE TESTER Used mostly in brownie and bar cookie baking, this is a thin, perfectly straight piece of wire which does not disturb the surface of the cookie when it is inserted. Doneness is determined according to the amount of crumbs left on the cake tester when it is removed.

COOKIE CUTTERS A basic set of different-size round cutters with fluted or plain edges is a good start. From there, hearts, stars, crescents, and, of course, the quintessential gingerbread man are all useful and make lovely cookies.

COOKIE SHEETS AND BAKING PANS
Without a doubt, the cookie sheet can mean the difference between success and failure. Invest in several heavy-gauge sheets with a minimum thickness of 1/8 inch. Heavy aluminum or coated steel will bake cookies properly without causing them to burn on the bottom (often the case with flimsy cookie sheets which do not conduct heat properly).

Other vital pans, those used for brownies and bar cookies, are: 8- or 9-inch square, 7 x 11 inches, 9 x 13 inches, and a jelly-roll pan. With the exception of the jelly-roll pan, which should be of shiny coated steel, metal or heavy aluminum, the baking pans can also be ovenproof glass, in which case, the oven temperature should be lowered by 25 degrees.

Two specialty pans are called for in a few of the recipes: A madeleine tray which has shell-like forms and a minimuffin tin with 12 molds measuring ¾ x 1¾ inches. Though seldom called for, they are essential to the following recipes: Madeleines (see page 114), Pecan Tartlets (see page 98) and Brownie Cups (see page 34).

COOLING RACKS Not to be confused with the racks in your oven, cooling racks should be large and sturdy with the wires close together. Always cool cookies in a single layer on racks before storing them.

DOUBLE BOILER Well worth the investment, it is a handy device for melting chocolate or chocolate and butter. A small, heavy saucepan placed in a slightly larger pan partially filled with simmering water works well; but you have to make certain that no water splashes into the chocolate.

ELECTRIC MIXER Though all stages of cookie making can be simply accomplished by hand, an electric mixer makes easy work of creaming butter and sugar. Beyond this step, it is recommended to retire the electric mixer and proceed by hand with a heavy wooden spoon.

NUT GRINDER Freshly ground nuts are wonderfully flavorful. If you have a food processor, put it to use and grind nuts a small amount at a time (as called for in the recipes), or invest a few extra dollars in a simple, hand-operated grinder; your cookies will show the difference in the place where it counts most . . . taste.

GRATERS For citrus zest, an ordinary kitchen grater works well. For grating nutmeg, a small, very sharp grater is made expressly for that purpose.

MOLDS AND PRESSES Molds make artistic creations of basic cookie dough. Certain cookies wouldn't be the same without them. Molds can be either carved wooden plaques or the rolling-pin type. Many holiday cookie recipes, especially from Germany and Scandinavia, call for molds as well as a cookie press, which makes a rich, buttery dough into stars, Christmas trees, wreaths or other shapes simply by changing the blade.

PASTRY BRUSH, TUBE, BAG AND BLENDER For brushing egg glazes on unbaked cookies, use a brush with nylon bristles or a feather. To pipe out soft, creamed doughs into evenly and imaginatively shaped cookies, use a pastry bag and tube. Tubes can be plain or star-shaped.

A pastry blender is a hand-held, dull-bladed device for cutting butter and flour together. Two kitchen knives held together can do the same job if you do not have one.

ROLLING PIN Dowel-type rolling pins are inevitably easier to handle, make quicker and easier work of rolling out dough and give you more control over rolling the dough to the thickness you want. However, rolling pins with handles achieve the same results.

SIFTER, STRAINER OR SIEVE Any of these three devices will sift flour and other dry ingredients together. The purpose of sifting is to aerate and break up any lumps in the flour.

SPOONS, SPATULAS AND SCRAPERS

Wooden spoons are used for creaming butter and sugar and for mixing eggs and dry ingredients into the creamed mixture. Scrapers, with both wide and narrow blades, are good for folding ingredients together as well as scraping every last bit of an ingredient from a pan. These are indispensable tools for cookie making.

Both a thin, flexible metal spatula and a wide-bladed turner are needed to remove various kinds of cookies from the cookie sheets.

VOLUME MEASURES

You will need a set of measuring spoons, measuring from ¼ teaspoon to 1 teaspoon, made of stainless steel (preferably) or molded hard plastic. Also needed is a set of graduated stainless-steel measuring cups for dry ingredients, holding ¼, ⅓, ½ and 1 cup measures. Glass measuring cups are used for liquids; a 1-cup size is usually sufficient.

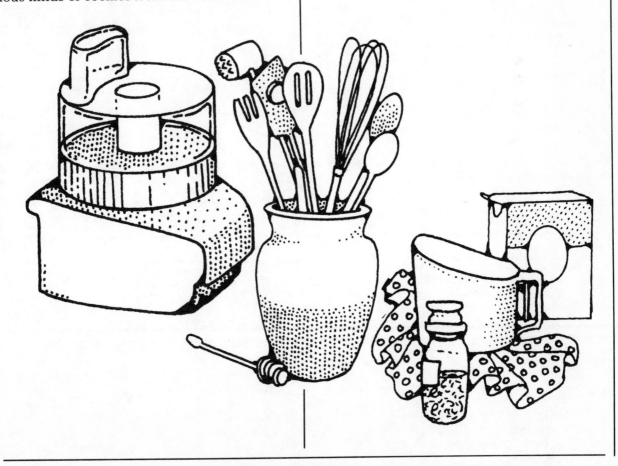

Cookie Basics

To make the very best cookies you must use the very best ingredients; but even with the finest chocolate, the freshest nuts and the creamiest butter, there are some tricks of the trade that will make your cookies better. Follow these tips and hints and you will bake perfect cookies every time.

MEASURING EXTRACTS Measure carefully when using any liquid flavoring, especially almond extract. It is very potent and when the cookies are baked you will know just how overpowering an extra amount can be.

MELTING CHOCOLATE Do this with caution. In the top pan of a double boiler over medium high heat or in a very heavy saucepan over low heat, chocolate will melt quite rapidly. It scorches easily, so be sure to remove it from the heat when it is *just* melted. Chocolate is also a tricky substance. An accidental drop of water can cause chocolate to become rough and lumpy. If this happens, don't throw it away, simply stir in 1 tablespoon of homogenized vegetable shortening for every 6 ounces of chocolate (the flavor of the chocolate will not be affected) and stir until it becomes smooth again.

Another method of melting chocolate is to place it in a saucepan in a low oven (250° F.) for 5 to 10 minutes.

GREASED COOKIE SHEETS Unsalted butter should be used to prepare cookie sheets, not vegetable oil or shortening, and not salted butter. Melt a small amount of butter and either paint it onto the cookie sheets with a pastry brush, or use a small piece of paper towel partially saturated in the butter. The cookie sheets should barely glisten with the butter; only a very thin layer is required to prevent cookies from sticking to the pan.

UNGREASED COOKIE SHEETS Butter the cookie sheets only when it is called for in the recipe. Many cookie doughs have a high butter content and, therefore, will not stick to the sheets.

"To this day 'cookie' is an Americanism; in England it is a biscuit, or simply a small cake. The American term probably came out of the contact of the English settlers with descendants of the Dutch of New Amsterdam, for 'cookie' is derived from Koejke, 'little cake.'"

AMELIA SIMMONS, orphan
American Cookery, 1796

21

COOLING MELTED INGREDIENTS

When chocolate, or chocolate and other ingredients, are melted together, they must be cooled to room temperature before adding them to creamed mixtures, especially with brownies.

CREAMING BUTTER Since the process of creaming butter forces air bubbles into it, always start with butter that has been brought to room temperature. Warm butter will take in more air bubbles than cold butter. Whether you're creaming the butter, or butter and sugar, by hand or with an electric mixer, it should be done vigorously until it becomes light, airy and creamy.

ADDING EGGS, FLAVORINGS AND FLOUR TO A CREAMED MIXTURE

Blend in eggs and flavorings quickly but thoroughly. Add the flour a little at a time. Stir in nuts and other heavier ingredients gently, almost folding rather than beating. Once the butter and sugar have been creamed, the intention is to keep as many air bubbles intact as possible, so be gentle with your creamed mixture!

BAKING COOKIES Never overload the oven. What you think you're gaining in time, you'll lose in quality. Good baking requires even heat circulating all around the pan. Most cookies bake best on the second rack from the bottom. Cookies baked near the top of the oven will have brown tops and uncooked bottoms.

MEASURING FLOUR AND OTHER DRY INGREDIENTS

Be sure to follow measurements exactly. Too much flour will result in dry, tough cookies. Spoon the flour loosely into the measuring cup and level with a spatula or the back of a straight knife. All-purpose flour has been presifted, and unless specified does not require resifting.

COOLING COOKIES Cool cookies in a single layer on a wire rack immediately after baking. Dropped, rolled, molded and pressed cookies are best removed from the cookie sheets with a wide spatula. Certain fragile cookies, like Florentine Tuiles, Pecan Lace Curls and Lacy Chocolate Chip Cookies may become difficult to remove from the pan; simply return the cookie sheet to the oven for a few seconds to resoften the cookies. Then, slide a thin metal spatula under the cookies and place them on cooling racks. Bar cookies and squares are usually cooled in the baking pan on a rack and cut after they have cooled.

STORING COOKIES To keep your cookies at the peak of perfection until every last crumb has been consumed, follow these simple rules: Store crisp cookies in containers with loose-fitting lids; store soft cookies in containers with tight, close-fitting lids. Soft cookies tend to dry out quickly, but a slice of apple in the container will ensure softness. Don't store crisp and soft cookies together; the crisp ones will get soggy. Any cookie made from dough with a high butter content should be refrigerated in an airtight container. Cookies that are to be kept for more than a week should be stored in the freezer (except meringues). Tightly wrapped in foil and in plastic freezer bags, they will last for up to 12 months without loss of flavor. Thaw for 15 minutes before serving. Bar cookies conveniently can be stored in their baking pan by covering it with a piece of plastic wrap and then foil; seal the edges tightly.

THE TEN COOKIE COMMANDMENTS

1. Use the finest-quality, freshest ingredients available.

2. Measure ingredients accurately and keep in mind that a slight change in the proportions of certain ingredients can change the consistency and texture of the dough dramatically.

3. Use liquid measuring cups for liquids and graduated measuring cups for dry ingredients.

4. Preheat your oven for 15 to 30 minutes before baking.

5. From time to time, check the temperature of your oven with an oven thermometer.

6. Strive to make all the cookies the same size, shape and thickness. Distribute them evenly and neatly on the cookie sheets and bake the cookies, 1 sheet at a time, in the center of the oven.

7. Check for doneness 2 minutes before the first time indicated in the recipe to avoid overbaking (a cookie's greatest foe).

8. Make sure the cookie sheets are completely cool before unbaked dough is placed on them or the butter in the dough will melt, the cookies will spread, and the ingredients will not bake together properly.

9. Use a minute timer for accuracy.

10. Remove the cookies from the baking sheet quickly (unless otherwise indicated). They continue to cook if left on piping-hot cookie sheets.

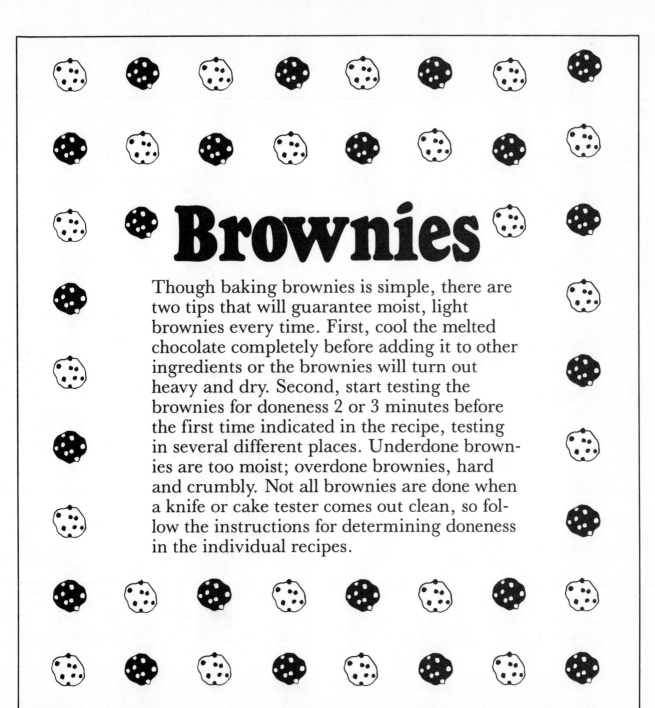

Brownies

Though baking brownies is simple, there are two tips that will guarantee moist, light brownies every time. First, cool the melted chocolate completely before adding it to other ingredients or the brownies will turn out heavy and dry. Second, start testing the brownies for doneness 2 or 3 minutes before the first time indicated in the recipe, testing in several different places. Underdone brownies are too moist; overdone brownies, hard and crumbly. Not all brownies are done when a knife or cake tester comes out clean, so follow the instructions for determining doneness in the individual recipes.

ALL-AMERICAN BROWNIES

Plain or fancy, there's nothing quite as delicious or memorable as a brownie. Using the highest-quality ingredients is the key to making this true American classic.

Makes 20 to 24 cookies

6 ounces (1½ sticks) butter
5 squares (5 ounces) unsweetened chocolate
1¼ cups all-purpose flour
1 teaspoon salt
1½ teaspoons baking powder
4 eggs
2 cups granulated sugar
1½ teaspoons vanilla extract
1 cup coarsely chopped walnuts

1. Preheat the oven to 350° F. Butter a 9- x 13-inch baking pan.

2. In a heavy saucepan over low heat, or in the top pan of a double boiler, melt the butter and chocolate together. Cool to room temperature.

3. Sift together the flour, salt and baking powder.

4. In a mixing bowl, beat the eggs and sugar together until thick and smooth.

5. Blend in the chocolate mixture and vanilla extract.

6. Add the flour mixture and stir until thoroughly combined; stir in the nuts.

7. Pour the batter into the buttered pan and smooth the top with a rubber spatula.

8. Bake for 25 to 30 minutes, or until sides pull away from the pan and a knife or cake tester inserted into the center has a few crumbs clinging to it when removed. Place the baking pan on a rack to cool completely before cutting into bars.

COCONUT BROWNIES. In place of the nuts, add 1 cup shredded coconut in step 6.

SUGAR AND SPICE BROWNIES. Substitute 2 cups vanilla sugar (see page 16) for granulated sugar; add 1 teaspoon ground cinnamon, ¼ teaspoon grated nutmeg and ⅛ teaspoon ground clove with the flour in step 3.

BLONDIES

Light and pale in color, these caramel-colored bar cookies are as rewarding to bake and serve as their distant cousin, the chocolate brownie.

Makes 30 cookies

6 ounces (1½ sticks) butter
1⅓ cups all-purpose flour
½ teaspoon salt
1 teaspoon baking powder
1¼ cups packed light brown sugar
2 eggs
1 teaspoon vanilla extract
1 cup coarsely chopped walnuts
½ cup coarsely chopped pecans

1. Preheat the oven to 375° F. Butter a 7¾- x 11½-inch baking pan.

2. In a heavy saucepan over low heat, or in the top pan of a double boiler, melt the butter. Cool to room temperature.

3. Sift together the flour, salt and baking powder.

4. In a large mixing bowl, beat the sugar and melted butter together until thick and smooth.

5. Beat in the eggs until thoroughly blended; add in the vanilla extract. Mix in the flour blending well. Stir in the nuts.

6. Pour the batter into the buttered pan and spread evenly with a rubber spatula.

7. Bake for 25 minutes, or until the sides pull away from the pan and a knife or cake tester inserted into the center comes out with a few moist crumbs clinging to it. Do not overbake.

8. Cool completely before cutting into bars.

MAPLE BLONDIES. At the end of step 4, add 2 tablespoons pure maple syrup and blend thoroughly.

CHOCOLATE CHIP NUT BLONDIES. Reduce walnuts to ½ cup and add 1 cup (6 ounces) semisweet chocolate chips at the end of step 5.

HOW MANY COOKIES IN A DOZEN?

If you're a baker, it's 13. How many cookies in a batch? It all depends on how rounded each teaspoon of batter is, how thick the dough is rolled out and how big (or small) you cut your brownies and bars. For these reasons, you could end up with a different number of cookies from that indicated in a recipe. So, consider the yield a "more or less" number of how many cookies to expect.

DOUBLE FUDGE BROWNIES

Deep, dark and rich in flavor and color, these brownies, with an extra burst of semisweet chocolate chips in every bite, will satisfy your chocolate cravings.

Makes 36 cookies

4 squares (4 ounces) unsweetened chocolate
8 ounces (2 sticks) butter
4 eggs
2 cups granulated sugar
2 teaspoons vanilla extract
1 ½ cups all-purpose flour
1 teaspoon baking powder
½ teaspoon salt
1 cup (6 ounces) semisweet chocolate chips

1. Preheat the oven to 350° F. Butter an 8 ¾- x 13 ½ -inch baking pan.

2. In a heavy saucepan over low heat, or in the top pan of a double boiler, melt the chocolate and butter together. Cool to room temperature.

3. In a large mixing bowl, beat the eggs and sugar until smooth and thick. Add the vanilla extract and melted chocolate mixture; blend well.

4. Mix the flour, baking powder and salt together. Add to the other ingredients, stirring until thoroughly combined. Stir in the chocolate chips.

5. Pour the mixture into the buttered baking pan. Bake for 25 to 30 minutes, or until the edges pull away from the sides of the pan. Cool completely before cutting into squares or bars.

NUT BROWNIES. Pour half of the batter into the pan. Evenly sprinkle 2 to 2 ½ cups coarsely chopped walnuts, pecans, almonds, or a mixture of nuts over the batter. Cover with the remaining batter and bake as directed.

BAKING PANS

Though brownies should always be tender, they can also be cakelike (high and light) or chewy (dense and moist). If you prefer chewy ones, use a 9- x 13-inch pan; for cakelike brownies, use a 9-inch-square baking pan.

Heat-resistant glass pans can also be used successfully when baking brownies, but reduce the oven temperature by 25° F. to avoid a tough crust.

CRISP BROWNIE COOKIES

Makes 45 to 50 cookies

8 squares (8 ounces) unsweetened chocolate
3 cups all-purpose flour
½ teaspoon baking soda
½ teaspoon ground cinnamon
¼ teaspoon salt
6 ounces (1 ½ sticks) butter
2 ½ cups packed dark brown sugar
2 eggs, lightly beaten
2 tablespoons water
1 teaspoon vanilla extract

1. Preheat the oven to 350° F. Butter cookie sheets.

2. In a heavy saucepan over low heat, or in the top pan of a double boiler, melt the chocolate. Cool to room temperature.

3. Sift together the flour, baking soda, cinnamon and salt.

4. Cream the butter and sugar until light and fluffy; beat in the eggs until well blended.

5. Mix in the cooled chocolate; then the water and vanilla extract. Add the flour mixture and beat until thoroughly combined.

6. Scrape the dough into a ball; chill for 15 minutes. Divide the dough into 4 equal parts. With your hand, roll the dough into logs about 1 ½ inches in diameter. Chill the logs for about 1 hour, or until firm. Cut off slices about ⅓ inch thick and place 1 ½ inches apart on the buttered sheets.

8. Bake for 10 to 12 minutes, or until the cookies are crisp on the bottom but soft to the touch. Cool completely on a rack.

FUDGE NUT BROWNIE COOKIES. At the end of step 5, stir in ¾ cup (4 ½ ounces) semisweet chocolate chips and ½ cup finely chopped pecans, walnuts or hazelnuts.

CHOCOLATE

Chocolate—that utterly desirable substance made up of chocolate liqueur, cocoa butter and sometimes sweetener—is frequently called for in two ways: unsweetened and sweetened. Baking chocolate that has no sweeteners added is intense in flavor and color; substituting sweetened for unsweetened chocolate in a recipe is not recommended. However, semisweet and bittersweet chocolates are interchangeable if your taste buds prefer. Milk chocolate makes great eating but unsatisfactory baking since it contains all kinds of other ingredients like milk solids, sugar and lecithin.

BLACK AND WHITE BROWNIES

Mildly tart yet very creamy, these brownies are somewhat reminiscent of chocolate cheesecake. Try serving them very cold or almost frozen.

Makes 16 cookies

Chocolate Batter
2 squares (2 ounces) unsweetened chocolate
1 square (1 ounce) semisweet chocolate
3 ounces (¾ stick) butter
½ cup all-purpose flour
½ teaspoon baking powder
¼ teaspoon salt
⅛ teaspoon ground cinnamon
¾ cup packed light brown sugar
1 egg, lightly beaten
½ teaspoon vanilla extract

Cream Cheese Batter
6 ounces cream cheese
¼ cup granuated sugar
1 egg
¼ teaspoon almond extract
2 tablespoons all-purpose flour, sifted twice

1. Preheat the oven to 325° F. Butter a 9-inch-square cake pan.

2. To prepare the chocolate batter, melt both kinds of chocolate and the butter together in a heavy saucepan or in the top pan of a double boiler over low heat. Cool to room temperature.

3. Sift the flour, baking powder, salt and cinnamon together.

4. Mix the brown sugar and egg together until thick and very smooth. Stir in the cooled chocolate mixture and vanilla extract. Add the flour mixture and stir until thoroughly combined.

5. To prepare cream cheese batter, use an electric mixer at low speed to beat the cream cheese and sugar together. Add the egg and almond extract, beating at moderate speed until the mixture is smooth. Add the sifted flour and continue beating only until the flour is blended.

6. Spread a thin layer of the chocolate batter on the bottom of the buttered baking pan. Make 4 mounds with the remaining chocolate mixture. Pour the cream cheese batter around and between the chocolate mounds. Using a table knife, swirl the batters together to create a marble pattern. Repeat the swirling motion in the opposite direction.

7. Bake for approximately 20 minutes, or until a knife or cake tester inserted into the center comes out clean. Cool completely, and refrigerate for 1 hour before cutting into squares.

AFTER-DINNER BROWNIES

An exciting and different approach to the brownie, this nut-flecked, finger-size confection is a cookie, a cake and a candy all in one. Liqueur-scented chocolate icings make these brownies perfect sweets to serve with coffee after a fine meal.

Makes 50 cookies

Brownie Batter

2 squares (2 ounces) unsweetened chocolate
2 squares (2 ounces) semisweet chocolate
3 ounces (¾ stick) butter
½ cup granulated sugar
1 egg
¼ cup light corn syrup
½ teaspoon vanilla extract
½ cup all-purpose flour
1 cup finely ground pecans

Icing

8 squares (8 ounces) semisweet chocolate
⅔ cup heavy cream
3 tablespoons liqueur (see Note)

Garnishes (see Note)

1. Preheat the oven to 350° F. Butter a 7½- x 11¾-inch baking pan.

2. In a heavy saucepan over low heat, or in the top pan of a double boiler, melt both kinds of chocolate and the butter together. Cool to room temperature.

3. Beat the sugar and egg together until thick and smooth. Add the corn syrup and vanilla, blending well. Stir in the flour and combine thoroughly. Mix in the ground nuts.

4. Pour the batter into the buttered baking pan and spread evenly with a rubber spatula. Bake for 20 to 25 minutes, or until sides pull away from pan and the mixture is completely set. A cake tester or knife inserted into the center should come away with a few moist crumbs still clinging. Cool the brownies on a rack before icing.

5. To prepare the icing, melt the chocolate and cream in a heavy saucepan over very low heat or in the top pan of a double boiler. When chocolate is barely melted, remove from the heat and stir with a spatula until smooth.

6. Strain the chocolate mixture through a fine sieve and cool to room temperature. Divide the icing into 3 equal parts and add a tablespoon of different liqueurs to each part, gently mixing well.

7. Divide the brownies into 3 equal sections with a sharp knife. With a thin metal spatula, spread a different liqueur-flavored icing evenly over each part. Garnish appropriately (see box). Place in the refrigerator and chill for approximately 2 hours, or until the icing is firm.

8. Cut each section into 5 lengthwise strips, and then into 1-inch bars. Refrigerated, they will keep nicely for up to 5 days.

Note: Liqueurs can be purchased in miniature single-serving size bottles, which will be enough for several batches of brownies.

TOPPING OFF AFTER-DINNER BROWNIES

Frost the brownies with liqueur-flavored icings and decorate with the corresponding garnishes.

LIQUEUR	GARNISH
Amaretto	Sliced Almond
Frangelica	Hazelnut
Coconut	Grated Coconut
Kahlúa	Candied Coffee Bean
Crème de Cassis	Raspberry
Rum or Brandy	Walnut
Bourbon	Pecan
Cointreau	Candied Orange Peel

BROWNIE CUPS

These fabulously fudgy little brownie tartlets look so lovely on a tray at coffee hour or teatime. The buttery cookie shell makes an interesting flavor, texture and color contrast to the intense, rum-flavored brownie filling.

Makes 36 cookies

Pastry

2 ounces (½ stick) butter
⅓ cup granulated sugar
1 egg
½ teaspoon vanilla extract
1½ cups all-purpose flour
¼ teaspoon salt
¼ teaspoon baking soda

Filling

2 squares (2 ounces) unsweetened chocolate
1½ squares (1½ ounces) semisweet chocolate
3 ounces (¾ stick) butter
½ cup packed dark brown sugar
½ cup light corn syrup
1 egg
1 tablespoon dark rum
⅓ cup all-purpose flour
⅛ teaspoon ground cinnamon
⅛ teaspoon salt
36 whole blanched almonds, toasted (see page 14) for garnish

1. To prepare the pastry, cream the butter and sugar together until light and fluffy.

2. Beat in the egg until well blended, then stir in the vanilla extract.

3. Sift the flour, salt and baking soda together. Stir into the creamed mixture, combining thoroughly. Gather the dough into a ball and wrap in foil or wax paper. Chill for about 2 hours, or until firm.

4. Butter 2 minimuffin tins. Roll the chilled dough to ¼-inch thickness or less. Using a 2¼-inch-round cookie cutter, stamp out the dough.

5. Fit each round into a mold, pressing lightly against the edges. Dough scraps can be rerolled if necessary. Refrigerate for 15 minutes before filling.

6. Preheat the oven to 375° F.

7. To prepare the filling, melt both kinds of chocolate and the butter in a heavy saucepan over low heat or in the top pan of a double boiler. Cool to room temperature. Blend the brown sugar and corn syrup together until smooth. Beat in the egg. Add the chocolate mixture, stirring until thoroughly combined. Mix in the rum.

8. Sift together the flour, cinnamon and salt; add to the chocolate mixture and stir until smooth.

9. Spoon the mixture into the chilled pastry,

about 1 tablespoon per mold; filling and pastry should be level. Place the minimuffin tins on a large baking sheet and bake for about 15 minutes, or until the pastry is golden and the filling is puffed. Immediately transfer minimuffin tins to a rack to cool.

10. While the brownie cups are still hot, place a blanched, toasted almond in the center of each, pressing down slightly. After 5 minutes, remove the brownie cups from the molds. Cool on the racks.

BROWNIE CUPS

Brownie cups require a minimuffin tin. This pan usually has 12 molds, measuring ¾ inch deep and 1¾ inches across the top. Once you have purchased this pan, put it to good use and make Pecan, Walnut or Macadamia Nut Tartlets (page 98) as well as Brownie Cups.

ESPRESSO BROWNIES

Besides the intense chocolate and coffee flavors, this unique brownie has an especially smooth and refined texture. The cappuccino version is lighter and creamier.

Makes 30 cookies

6 tablespoons instant espresso powder
2 tablespoons boiling water
4 ounces (1 stick) butter
3 squares (3 ounces) unsweetened chocolate
1 square (1 ounce) semisweet chocolate
¾ cup all-purpose flour
¼ teaspoon salt
½ teaspoon baking powder
1¼ cups packed light brown sugar
2 eggs
1 teaspoon vanilla extract
½ teaspoon almond extract
¼ cup heavy cream

1. Preheat the oven to 375° F. Butter a 7¾- x 11½-inch baking pan.

2. Dissolve the espresso powder in the boiling water.

3. In a heavy saucepan over low heat, or in the top pan of a double boiler, melt the butter and both kinds of chocolate together. Cool to room temperature.

4. Sift the flour, salt and baking powder together.

5. In a large mixing bowl, beat the brown sugar and eggs until thick and smooth. Stir in the chocolate mixture, blending thoroughly.

6. Add the dissolved espresso powder and mix well. Stir in the vanilla extract, almond extract and heavy cream. Blend in the flour mixture, stirring until thoroughly combined.

7. Pour the mixture into the buttered baking pan. Bake for 20 to 25 minutes, or until the sides pull away from the pan and a knife inserted into the center comes out clean. Cool the pan on a rack. Cut into bars when completely cool. Serve cold or partially frozen for a chewier texture.

CAPPUCCINO BROWNIES. In step 2 reduce espresso powder to 3 tablespoons.

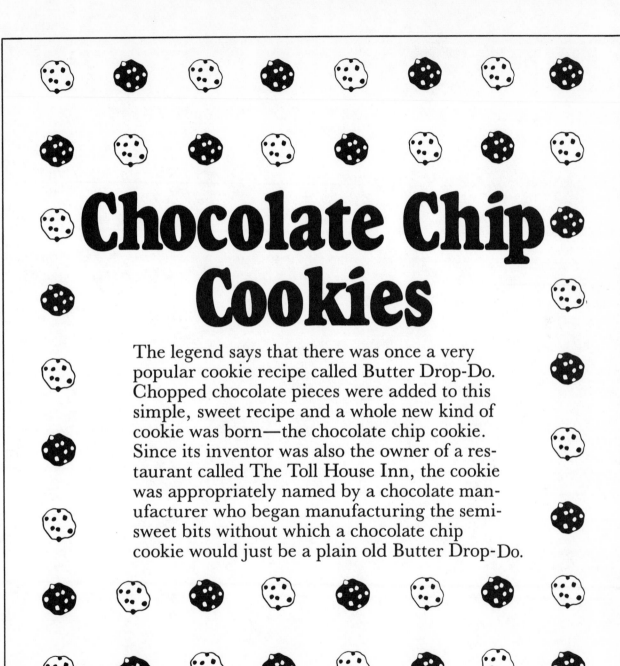

Chocolate Chip Cookies

The legend says that there was once a very popular cookie recipe called Butter Drop-Do. Chopped chocolate pieces were added to this simple, sweet recipe and a whole new kind of cookie was born—the chocolate chip cookie. Since its inventor was also the owner of a restaurant called The Toll House Inn, the cookie was appropriately named by a chocolate manufacturer who began manufacturing the semisweet bits without which a chocolate chip cookie would just be a plain old Butter Drop-Do.

THE TOLL HOUSE COOKIE

The chocolate chip cookie is one of America's most creative and delicious culinary inventions. You can't miss with "the original" and its wealth of variations.

Makes 65 to 70 cookies

2¼ cups all-purpose flour
1 teaspoon baking soda
1 teaspoon salt
8 ounces (2 sticks) butter
¾ cup granulated sugar
¾ cup packed brown sugar
2 eggs, lightly beaten
1 teaspoon vanilla extract
2 cups (12 ounces) semisweet chocolate chips

1. Preheat the oven to 375° F. Butter cookie sheets.

2. Combine the flour, baking soda and salt.

3. In a large mixing bowl, cream the butter and both sugars until light and fluffy.

4. Beat in the eggs until the mixture is smooth and well blended; stir in the vanilla extract.

5. Gradually add the flour mixture, beating until thoroughly combined. Stir in the chocolate chips.

6. Drop the batter by rounded teaspoons about 1½ inches apart onto the buttered cookie sheets. Bake for 8 to 10 minutes, or until the cookies are brown around the edges but still slightly soft in the centers. Cool on a rack.

CRISP CHOCOLATE CHIP COOKIES. In step 4, add 2 tablespoons cold water.

CAKELIKE CHOCOLATE CHIP COOKIES. Use 3 eggs. In step 2, add ¼ teaspoon baking powder.

PEANUT BUTTER CHOCOLATE CHIP COOKIES. Reduce butter to 4 ounces (1 stick). At the end of step 3, blend in ⅔ cup extra-crunchy peanut butter.

COCONUT CHOCOLATE CHIP COOKIES. At the end of step 5, add 1 cup shredded coconut.

NUTTY CHOCOLATE CHIP COOKIES. Add 1 cup chopped walnuts, hazelnuts, pecans or unsalted peanuts at the end of step 5.

VERY NUTTY CHOCOLATE CHIP COOKIES. Add 1 cup coarsely chopped toasted walnuts (see page 14) and ½ cup ground pecans at the end of step 5.

RAISIN NUT CHOCOLATE CHIP COOK-IES. Add ½ cup chopped walnuts, pecans, hazelnuts or the nut of your choice along with ½ cup raisins at the end of step 5.

CHOCOLATE CHIP COOKIE BARS. Butter a 10- x 15-inch jelly-roll pan; spread in the dough and smooth with a rubber spatula. Bake in the middle of the oven for 20 minutes. Cool in the pan. Makes 35 two-inch squares.

GIANT CHOCOLATE CHIP COOKIES

These days, there's more to consider than just taste when it comes to chocolate chip cookies. We've grown more sophisticated, or perhaps just more demanding. When the cry for cookies is "make them large," here is the foolproof method.

Prepare the cookie dough as directed. Measure ¼ cup of dough for each cookie. Place the mounds of dough 4 inches apart on a buttered cookie sheet and shape into 2½-inch rounds. Bake for 11 to 13 minutes. Makes 18 cookies.

OATMEAL CHOCOLATE CHIP COOKIES

Makes 55 to 60 cookies

1 cup flour
½ teaspoon baking powder
¼ teaspoon salt
6 ounces (1½ sticks) butter, at room temperature
½ cup granulated sugar
½ cup packed dark brown sugar
1 egg, lightly beaten
1 teaspoon vanilla
1 cup quick-cooking (*not* instant) oats
1⅓ cups (8 ounces) semisweet chocolate chips

1. Preheat the oven to 350° F. Butter cookie sheets.

2. Sift the flour, baking powder and salt together.

3. In a mixing bowl, cream the butter and both sugars until light and fluffy.

4. Add the egg and blend well; stir in the vanilla extract. Add in the flour mixture and combine thoroughly. Stir in the oats and chocolate chips.

5. Drop the dough by heaping teaspoons 2½ inches apart onto the buttered cookie sheets. Bake for 10 to 12 minutes, or until the edges of the cookies are lacy and lightly browned. Cool on a rack.

DOUBLE ALMOND CHOCOLATE CHIP COOKIES

Chocolate and almonds have long been paired in the culinary arts. This light and cakelike cookie, with the crunch of toasted almonds and semisweet chocolate chips, is a lovely fusion of these two complementary flavors.

Makes 45 to 50 cookies

2 cups all-purpose flour
1 teaspoon baking soda
1 teaspoon salt
½ teaspoon ground cinnamon
8 ounces (2 sticks) butter
1½ cups packed light brown sugar
2 whole eggs, lightly beaten
2 extra egg yolks, lightly beaten
2 teaspoons vanilla extract
1 teaspoon almond extract
2 cups (12 ounces) semisweet chocolate chips
1⅓ cups slivered almonds, toasted
   (see page 14)

1. Preheat the oven to 350° F. Butter cookie sheets.

2. Sift the flour, baking soda, salt and cinnamon together.

3. In a large mixing bowl, cream the butter and brown sugar until light and fluffy.

4. Beat in the whole eggs and egg yolks until well blended; stir in the vanilla and almond extracts.

5. Add the flour mixture and stir until thoroughly combined. Stir in the chocolate chips and toasted almonds.

6. Drop the batter by level tablespoons 3 inches apart onto the buttered cookie sheets. Bake for 8 to 10 minutes, or until the edges are brown and the centers are still slightly soft.

7. Cool on the sheets for 1 minute. Using a wide spatula, remove the cookies to racks to cool completely.

TOFFEE CHOCOLATE CHIP COOKIES

Makes 45 to 50 cookies

2 cups all-purpose flour
1 teaspoon baking soda
½ teaspoon salt
¼ teaspoon grated nutmeg
8 ounces (2 sticks) butter
2 cups packed dark brown sugar
2 eggs, lightly beaten
1½ teaspoons vanilla extract
1 cup (6 ounces) semisweet chocolate chips
1½ cups ground pecans

1. Preheat the oven to 375° F. Butter cookie sheets.

2. Sift the flour, baking soda, salt and nutmeg together.

3. In a medium-size mixing bowl, cream the butter and sugar until light and fluffy.

4. Beat in the eggs; stir in the vanilla extract.

5. Add the flour mixture and stir until thoroughly combined. Fold in the chocolate chips and pecans.

6. Drop the batter by level tablespoons 2 inches apart onto the buttered cookie sheets.

7. Bake for 8 to 10 minutes, or until the edges are browned and the centers are almost firm to the touch. Remove cookies to a rack to cool.

BOURBON TOFFEE CHOCOLATE CHIP COOKIES. Add ⅓ cup bourbon at the end of step 4.

ICEBOX CHOCOLATE CHIP COOKIES

These crisp, thin, chocolate chip cookies are for people who love them fresh from the oven. Tightly wrapped, the dough can be kept frozen for at least a month.

Makes 35 to 40 cookies

1½ cups all-purpose flour
¼ teaspoon salt
¼ teaspoon baking soda
4 ounces (1 stick) butter
½ cup granulated sugar
½ cup packed dark brown sugar
1 egg, lightly beaten
½ teaspoon vanilla extract
½ cup (3 ounces) semisweet chocolate chips, coarsely chopped

1. Preheat the oven to 375° F. 15 to 30 minutes before you are ready to bake the cookies. Butter cookie sheets.

2. Sift the flour, salt and baking soda together.

3. In a mixing bowl, cream the butter and both sugars until light and fluffy.

4. Beat in the egg until well blended; stir in the vanilla extract.

5. Add the flour mixture, stirring until thoroughly combined. Fold in the chocolate chips. The dough will be soft.

6. Scrape the dough into a ball and cover with foil. Chill for 45 minutes, or until firm enough to shape.

7. Shape the dough into two 5-inch logs approximately 2 inches in diameter. Wrap each log in foil and freeze until ready to bake.

8. With a sharp knife cut the dough into ¼-inch slices. Place 2 inches apart on the buttered cookie sheets and bake for 10 to 12 minutes, or until the cookies are well browned. Cool cookies on a rack.

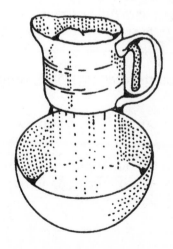

43

DOUBLE AND TRIPLE CHOCOLATE CHOCOLATE CHIPS

The "double" is definitely for chocolate lovers. The "triple" is for chocolaholics!

Makes 45 to 50 cookies

⅓ cup Dutch-process cocoa
1⅓ cups all-purpose flour
¼ teaspoon baking soda
½ teaspoon salt
6 ounces (1½ sticks) butter
1 cup granulated sugar
1 egg, lightly beaten
1½ teaspoons vanilla extract
1 cup (6 ounces) semisweet chocolate chips

1. Preheat the oven to 375° F. Butter cookie sheets.

2. Sift the cocoa, flour, baking soda and salt together.

3. Cream the butter and sugar until light and fluffy. Beat in the egg and blend well; stir in the vanilla extract.

4. Blend in the flour mixture until thoroughly combined. Add chocolate chips. Drop the dough by level tablespoons 1½ inches apart onto the buttered cookie sheets.

5. Bake for 8 to 10 minutes, or until the cookies are brown around the edges but still slightly soft in the center. Using a wide spatula, remove the cookies to a rack to cool.

TRIPLE CHOCOLATE CHIP COOKIES.

In a heavy saucepan over low heat, or in the top pan of a double boiler, melt 4 squares (4 ounces) semisweet chocolate. Cool to room temperature. At the end of step 3, add the cooled chocolate, stirring until well blended. In step 5, allow the cookies to cool on the cookie sheet for 2 to 3 minutes before removing to a rack to cool.

WHOLE-WHEAT AND HONEY CHOCOLATE CHIP COOKIES

Whole-wheat flour makes these cookies denser and more cakelike.

Makes 45 to 50 cookies

2 cups whole-wheat flour
¼ teaspoon baking soda
½ teaspoon salt
½ teaspoon ground cinnamon
4 ounces (1 stick) butter
1 cup honey
1 teaspoon vanilla extract
2 eggs, lightly beaten
1⅓ cups (8 ounces) semisweet chocolate
   chips
½ cup coarsely chopped walnuts, toasted (see
   page 14)

1. Preheat the oven to 350° F. Butter cookie sheets.

2. Sift the flour, baking soda, salt and cinnamon together.

3. Cream the butter until fluffy; stir in the honey and vanilla extract.

4. Beat in the eggs until well blended. Gradually add the flour mixture, stirring until thoroughly combined. Add the chocolate chips and walnuts.

5. Drop batter by heaping teaspoons 1½ inches apart onto the buttered cookie sheets. Bake for 15 to 18 minutes, or until the cookies are well browned on the bottoms. Cool on a rack.

LACY CHOCOLATE CHIP COOKIES

Besides being slightly sweeter than the other chocolate chip cookies in this book, these are also more fragile, more delicate and crispier.

Makes 35 to 40 cookies

3 ounces (¾ stick) butter
½ cup all-purpose flour
¼ teaspoon salt
¼ teaspoon baking soda
3 tablespoons packed light brown sugar
3 tablespoons granulated sugar
¼ teaspoon vanilla extract
¼ cup finely chopped walnuts
⅓ cup (2 ounces) semisweet chocolate chips

1. Preheat the oven to 375° F. Lightly butter cookie sheets.

2. In a heavy saucepan over low heat, or in the top pan of a double boiler, melt the butter and cool to room temperature.

3. Sift the flour, salt and baking soda together.

4. Combine both sugars and the melted butter, stirring until smooth. Add the vanilla extract and mix well. Add the flour mixture beating until all the ingredients are combined thoroughly. Mix in the nuts and chocolate chips.

5. Drop the batter by level teaspoons 3 inches apart onto the buttered cookie sheets.

6. Bake for 6 to 8 minutes or until cookies are lacy and a rich caramel color.

7. Cool on the cookie sheet for 1 minute. Using a wide spatula, remove the cookies to a rack to cool completely.

Bar Cookies

Bar cookies have two wonderful attributes—speed and simplicity. Just make a dough, spread it into a pan and bake. They may be cakelike cookies or layered with different textures, such as chopped nuts, sweet pastry dough, coconut or spicy fruit fillings. Cut them as large or as small as you like.

ALMOND LEMON SQUARES

These bars are light as a feather. A buttery base complements the crunchy almond and lemon topping. They go especially well with hot tea.

Makes 16 cookies

Lemon Batter
4 ounces (1 stick) butter
⅓ cup granulated sugar
⅓ cup packed light brown sugar
2 egg yolks
¼ cup fresh lemon juice
¼ cup heavy cream
1⅓ cups flour
¼ teaspoon salt
½ teaspoon baking powder

Almond Topping
1¼ cups sliced blanched almonds
2 tablespoons packed light brown sugar
grated zest from 1 large lemon, about 2 teaspoons
2 tablespoons butter

1. Preheat the oven to 350° F. Butter a 9-inch-square baking pan.

2. In a heavy saucepan over very low heat, melt the butter for both topping and batter (4 ounces plus 2 tablespoons).

3. To prepare the lemon batter, mix ½ cup of the melted butter and both sugars together. Blend in the egg yolks. Stir in the lemon juice and cream, mixing until thoroughly combined.

4. Sift together the flour, salt and baking powder and combine with the sugar and yolk mixture.

5. Pour the batter into the buttered baking pan; make an even layer with a rubber spatula. Set aside.

6. To prepare the almond topping, combine the almonds, brown sugar and lemon zest. Add remaining 2 tablespoons melted butter and mix well.

7. Cover the lemon batter evenly with the almond topping mixture.

8. Bake for 20 to 25 minutes, or until edges pull away from the pan and a cake tester inserted into the center comes out with moist crumbs clinging to it. Do not overbake.

9. Place the pan on a rack to cool. When completely cooled, cut into squares.

CHEWY HAZELNUT BARS

A light, cookie crust is covered with a meringuelike, hazelnut mixture. The outcome is a nut bar reminiscent of a candy—very chewy and crunchy.

Makes 45 to 50 cookies

Batter

6 ounces (1½ sticks) butter
3 egg yolks
1½ teaspoons rum extract
2 cups confectioners' sugar
1½ cups all-purpose flour
½ cup cornstarch
¼ teaspoon salt

Topping

2 cups (7½ ounces) chopped hazelnuts
2 tablespoons light corn syrup
2 tablespoons packed light brown sugar
3 egg whites

1. Preheat the oven to 325° F. Lightly butter a 10- x 15-inch jelly-roll pan.

2. Cream the butter. Beat in the egg yolks and rum extract. Stir in the confectioners' sugar, combining thoroughly.

3. Sift the flour, cornstarch and salt together.

Add to the creamed mixture and stir until just blended.

4. Press the batter into the buttered baking pan, making an even layer. Bake for 15 minutes. While this is baking, prepare the topping by mixing the hazelnuts, corn syrup and light brown sugar together.

5. In a small bowl, beat the egg whites until soft peaks form; fold into the nut mixture.

6. After the bars have baked for 15 minutes, remove the pan and increase the oven temperature to 375° F. Spread the topping mixture over the partially baked bars, making a smooth layer. Return the pan to the oven and bake for 15 minutes more, or until the nuts are golden brown. Cool on a rack. Cut into bars while still warm.

RUM RAISIN SQUARES

An interesting interpretation of a long-standing flavor duo, these delicious soft and spicy bar cookies have rum-soaked raisins throughout and a crackly butter rum icing on top.

Makes 16 cookies

Batter

2½ ounces (⅝ stick) butter
¼ cup plus 2 tablespoons packed light brown
    sugar
1 cup dark raisins
¼ cup dark rum
½ teaspoon vanilla extract
¾ cup all-purpose flour
½ teaspoon salt
¼ teaspoon baking soda
½ teaspoon ground cinnamon
⅛ teaspoon grated nutmeg

Butter Rum Icing

⅓ cup confectioners' sugar
2 teaspoons rum
1 tablespoon butter

1. Preheat the oven to 325° F. Lightly butter a 9-inch-square baking pan.

2. In a small mixing bowl, combine 1 tablespoon of the butter, 2 tablespoons of the light brown sugar, the raisins and the rum. Let the mixture stand for 30 minutes.

3. Cream remaining 2 ounces butter and the ¼ cup sugar together until light and smooth. Mix in the vanilla extract.

4. Sift the flour, salt, baking soda, cinnamon and nutmeg together. Stir into the creamed mixture and combine thoroughly; add the raisin mixture, blending well.

5. Scrape the mixture into the buttered baking pan, making an even layer with a rubber spatula. Bake for about 20 minutes, or until the edges pull away from the pan and a knife or cake tester inserted into the center comes out clean. Cool on a rack.

6. To prepare the butter-rum icing, mix the confectioners' sugar and rum together. Add the butter and blend until very smooth. Spread over the cooled cake. After the icing has set, about 1 hour, cut into squares.

FRUITCAKE BARS

This recipe could easily become a holiday classic around your house. Even people who turn up their noses at fruitcake find this crispy-bottom, chewy-top bar surprisingly delectable. Glistening with red and green candied cherries, these cookies make wonderful edible gifts when wrapped in colored cellophane and tied with a ribbon.

Makes 36 cookies

Cookie Crust

2 cups all-purpose flour
½ teaspoon salt
¼ cup packed dark brown sugar
6 ounces (1½ sticks) butter
2 egg yolks
1 tablespoon brandy

Fruit and Nut Topping

½ cup dark raisins
½ cup mixed candied fruits, finely chopped
2 tablespoons brandy
½ cup coarsely chopped pecans
⅓ cup slivered blanched almonds
½ cup granulated sugar
¼ cup dark corn syrup
½ teaspoon vanilla extract
2 eggs, lightly beaten
18 candied cherries, halved

1. Preheat the oven to 375° F. 15 to 30 minutes before you are ready to bake the cookies. Lightly butter a cake pan 13 x 9 x 2 inches.

2. To prepare the cookie crust, combine the flour, salt and brown sugar together until thoroughly blended.

3. Cut the butter into small pieces and, using your fingertips, rub it into the flour mixture until the mixture resembles oatmeal.

4. Beat the egg yolks and 1 tablespoon brandy together; pour over the flour mixture. Using a fork, blend until the pastry is evenly moistened and crumbly; do not overmix. Press the cookie crust evenly into the buttered baking pan. Chill for 30 minutes.

5. Combine the raisins, candied fruits and 2 tablespoons brandy. Let stand for 15 minutes.

6. Mix together the pecans and almonds with the raisins and candied fruits in the brandy. Stir in the sugar, corn syrup and vanilla extract; beat in the eggs.

"A woman with shorn white hair is standing at the kitchen window. 'Oh my,' she exclaims, her breath smoking the windowpane, 'it's fruitcake weather!' "

TRUMAN CAPOTE
A Christmas Memory

7. Bake the cookie crust for 15 minutes. Remove the cookie crust from the oven and spread on the fruitcake topping, using a spatula to make an even layer. Decorate with candied cherries, making 6 rows of 6 cherries.

8. Return to the oven and bake for 15 more minutes, or until the topping is set. Cool the pan on a rack. When completely cooled, cut into bars.

CHOCOLATE COCONUT SLICES

This is a moist bar, thick with chewy coconut, that takes only a few minutes to prepare. The slices stay deliciously fresh for a week, or more when refrigerated or frozen.

Makes 45 to 50 cookies

6 squares (6 ounces) semisweet chocolate
1 ounce (¼ stick) plus 4 ounces (1 stick)
    butter
2 cups shredded coconut
1½ cups granulated sugar
2 eggs
½ teaspoon almond extract
½ cup Dutch-process cocoa powder
1½ cups all-purpose flour
½ teaspoon salt

1. Preheat the oven to 325° F. Butter a 10- x 15-inch jelly-roll pan.

2. In a small saucepan over low heat, or in the top pan of a double boiler, melt the chocolate. Remove the chocolate from the heat and swirl in 1 ounce of the butter. After the butter is blended in, add the coconut. Cool to room temperature.

3. Cream the remaining 4 ounces butter and the sugar until light and fluffy. Beat in the eggs until just blended; stir in the almond extract.

4. Sift the cocoa, flour and salt together; stir into the creamed mixture until thoroughly combined. Blend in the cooled chocolate mixture.

5. Pour the mixture into the buttered jelly-roll pan and smooth with a palette knife or rubber spatula. Bake for 18 to 20 minutes, or until the sides pull away from the pan and a cake tester inserted into the center comes out almost clean. Cool on a rack before cutting into slices.

DATE NUT BARS

Really fresh dates are soft when you buy them; baking does not make them soft. What's more, the fresher the dates, the more intense the taste of your date nut bars! Try California Medjool dates (see Mail-Order Guide, page 119, for sources).

Makes 20 to 25 cookies

Batter
6 ounces (1½ sticks) butter
3 cups pitted dates, coarsely chopped
1⅓ cups light brown sugar
1 teaspoon vanilla extract
1 teaspoon almond extract
2 cups all-purpose flour
½ teaspoon salt
1 teaspoon baking powder
¼ teaspoon ground cloves
½ cup heavy cream
1½ cups coarsely chopped walnuts

Topping
½ cup quick-cooking (*not* instant) oats
¼ cup all-purpose flour
⅓ cup packed light brown sugar
¾ cup walnuts, finely chopped
2 tablespoons butter

1. Preheat the oven to 350° F. Butter a shallow 13- x 9- x 2-inch baking pan.

2. In a heavy saucepan over low heat, melt the butter. Cool slightly.

3. Combine the melted butter, chopped dates, brown sugar, vanilla and almond extracts together. Let stand for 15 minutes.

4. Sift the flour, salt, baking powder and cloves together.

5. Stir the cream into the date mixture. Add the flour mixture, stirring until thoroughly combined. Mix in the walnuts.

6. Spread the mixture evenly into the buttered baking pan.

7. To prepare the topping, mix the oats, flour, brown sugar and walnuts together. Add the butter and blend with your hands until crumbly. Sprinkle the topping evenly over the batter.

8. Bake for 20 to 25 minutes, or until a knife inserted into the center comes out clean. Cool on a rack. When completely cooled, cut into bars.

APRICOT NUT BARS. Substitute 3 cups dried apricots, coarsely chopped, for the dates.

SPICE BARS

Take advantage of the goodies on your spice rack. These quickly assembled bars have a soft, chewy texture and an old-fashioned spice cake flavor.

Makes 15 cookies

1 cup all-purpose flour
½ teaspoon baking soda
¼ teaspoon salt
1½ teaspoons ground cinnamon
½ teaspoon ground allspice
¼ teaspoon ground ginger
4 ounces (1 stick) butter
⅔ cup granulated sugar
1 egg, lightly beaten
¼ cup molasses
½ teaspoon vanilla extract
2 tablespoons white crystal sugar

1. Preheat the oven to 325° F. Butter and lightly flour a 9-inch-square baking pan.

2. Sift together the flour, baking soda, salt, cinnamon, allspice and ginger.

3. Cream the butter and sugar until light and fluffy. Beat in the egg. Stir in the molasses and vanilla extract; blend well.

4. Stir in the flour mixture until thoroughly combined. Scrape the mixture into the baking pan and smooth evenly with a rubber spatula.

5. Sprinkle an even layer of crystal sugar over the batter. Bake for 20 to 25 minutes, or until edges pull away from the pan and a knife or cake tester inserted 1 inch from the edge comes away clean. Do not overbake. Cool on a rack. Cut into bars when completely cool. They will sink slightly while cooling.

ORANGE ICED SPICE BARS. Add the grated zest from 1 medium-size orange (about 2 teaspoons) at the end of step 3. Bake as directed, omitting the sugar crystals. Cool completely. To prepare the orange icing, combine 2 tablespoons orange-juice concentrate with 2 teaspoons hot water and ½ cup sifted confectioners' sugar. Blend well. After the spice cake has cooled completely, spread the icing evenly over the top. Allow the icing to set completely, about 1 hour, before cutting into bars.

Rolled Cookies

Cookies made from rolled dough are thin and crisp. They are also among the most attractive cookies when cut with interestingly shaped cookie cutters. This type of dough is easier to work with when it is well chilled and only a small amount is rolled at a time.

The cookies should always be "stamped out" as close together as possible. The scraps can be rerolled, but the cookies made from the rerolled dough will never be as tender as those from once-rolled dough.

To begin, roll the dough on a lightly floured work surface (a board, slab of marble or a pastry cloth). Dip the cookie cutter into flour or sugar each time before cutting to prevent sticking; however, use as little additional flour as possible as this toughens the dough.

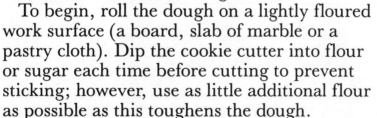

ISCHLER HEARTS

Laced with apricot jam and dipped into a rich chocolate glaze, Ischler Hearts begin with a classic Viennese cookie dough. If you don't have a heart-shaped cookie cutter, any shape will do.

Makes 25 to 30 cookies

Cookie Dough
12 ounces (3 sticks) butter
3 ounces cream cheese
1½ cups granulated sugar
1 egg, lightly beaten
2 cups all-purpose flour
½ teaspoon salt
1½ teaspoons grated orange zest
1½ cups ground blanched almonds
½ cup apricot jam

Glaze
8 squares (8 ounces) semisweet chocolate
3 tablespoons butter
⅓ cup heavy cream
1 teaspoon rum extract

1. Preheat the oven to 350° F. Butter cookie sheets.

2. Cream the butter until smooth and soft; beat in the cream cheese, sugar and egg, blending well.

3. Sift the flour and salt together and stir into the creamed mixture. Stir in the orange zest; fold in the almonds.

4. Divide the dough into halves. Roll out one portion of the dough on a sugared work surface to ⅛-inch thickness, using more sugar as necessary to prevent the dough from sticking. With a 1½-inch heart-shaped cookie cutter, stamp out the cookies and transfer to the buttered cookie sheets. Repeat with remaining dough and scraps.

5. Bake the cookies for 8 to 10 minutes, or until they are firm and the bottoms are a light golden brown. Remove to racks to cool completely.

6. Warm the apricot jam and spread a thin layer on half of the cookies. Cover each with a plain cookie.

7. To prepare the chocolate glaze, melt the chocolate, butter and heavy cream in the top pan of a double boiler or in a heavy saucepan over very low heat. Cool slightly; stir in the rum extract. Dip each cookie lengthwise halfway into the chocolate mixture and place on cookie sheets lined with wax paper. Refrigerate for 1 hour, or until set. Store the cookies between layers of wax paper in the refrigerator.

BLACK BOTTOMS

Crisp butter cookies painted with a layer of semisweet or bittersweet chocolate, then coated with fancy Brazil or pistachio nuts—these are particularly elegant dessert cookies.

Makes 25 to 30 cookies

8 ounces (2 sticks) butter
⅔ cup granulated sugar
2 eggs, lightly beaten
2 teaspoons rum extract
2 teaspoons grated orange zest
2⅔ cups all-purpose flour
½ teaspoon salt
6 squares (6 ounces) semisweet or bittersweet chocolate
¾ cup coarsely chopped Brazil or pistachio nuts

1. Preheat the oven to 350° F. 15 to 30 minutes before you are ready to bake the cookies. Butter cookie sheets.

2. Cream the butter and sugar until light and fluffy.

3. Beat in the eggs, rum extract and orange zest.

4. Sift the flour and salt together; stir into the creamed mixture until thoroughly combined.

5. Gather the dough into a ball; chill for about 2 hours, or until firm.

6. Divide the dough into halves. Using a lightly floured work surface, roll out one portion of the dough to ⅜-inch thickness. With a 2½-inch-round cookie cutter, stamp out the cookies and transfer to the buttered cookie sheets. Refrigerate the scraps for a few minutes and repeat the procedure.

7. Bake the cookies for 10 to 12 minutes, or until firm to the touch and lightly browned on the bottom. Cool on a rack.

8. To make the chocolate coating, melt the chocolate in a heavy saucepan over low heat or in the top pan of a double boiler. Cool to room temperature.

9. When the cookies have cooled completely, paint one side with a thin layer of melted chocolate. Press the cookies into the chopped nuts. Chill for 1 hour, or until the nuts are firmly set into the chocolate.

LINZER COOKIES

These classic Austrian cookies are made of 2 buttery cookie mounds sandwiched together with raspberry jam and generously dusted with confectioners' sugar.

Makes 25 to 30 cookies

8 ounces (2 sticks) butter
1 cup granulated sugar
1 egg
1 teaspoon vanilla extract
2½ cups all-purpose flour
½ teaspoon salt
⅛ teaspoon ground cloves
1 cup finely chopped walnuts
1 cup raspberry jam
½ cup confectioners' sugar

1. Preheat the oven to 375° F. Butter cookie sheets.

2. Cream the butter and sugar together. Beat in the egg; stir in the vanilla extract.

3. Sift the flour, salt and cloves together. Beat into the creamed mixture until well blended; stir in the walnuts. Chill the dough for about 30 minutes, or until firm.

4. Divide the dough into halves. On a lightly floured work surface, roll out one half of the dough to ⅜-inch thickness, using additional flour as necessary to prevent the dough from sticking.

5. With a 2-inch-round cutter, stamp out the cookies. Then, using a 1-inch-round cookie cutter, stamp the centers out of half of the cookies; these will be the cookie tops. Chill the scraps and reroll. Place on the buttered cookie sheets 1½ inches apart.

6. Bake the tops and bottoms for 7 to 9 minutes, or until the cookies are pale, yet firm to the touch. Cool on a rack.

7. When completely cool, spread each cookie bottom with 1 tablespoon of raspberry jam. Dip each cookie top into confectioners' sugar and lightly place it—sugared side up—on top of the half with raspberry jam. Add additional jam to fill up the centers.

8. Store in an airtight container between layers of wax paper.

GINGERBREAD MEN

Makes 20 to 24 cookies, using a 5-inch cookie cutter

3 cups all-purpose flour
½ teaspoon baking soda
½ teaspoon salt
2 teaspoons ground ginger
1 teaspoon ground cinnamon
½ teaspoon ground cloves
¼ teaspoon grated nutmeg
4 ounces (1 stick) butter
⅔ cup packed light brown sugar
½ cup dark molasses
1 egg, lightly beaten

1. Preheat the oven to 375° F. 15 to 30 minutes before you are ready to bake the cookies. Butter cookie sheets.

2. Sift the flour, baking soda, salt, ginger, cinnamon, cloves and nutmeg together.

3. Cream the butter and sugar until smooth and light. Blend in the molasses and the egg.

4. Stir the dry ingredients into the creamed mixture until thoroughly combined.

5. Gather the dough into a ball and knead it 2 or 3 times, or until smooth. Wrap in wax paper and chill for 4 to 6 hours, or until very firm.

6. Divide the dough into halves. On a lightly floured surface, roll to ⅛-inch thickness. Using a cookie cutter dipped into flour, stamp out the gingerbread men. Using a wide metal spatula, transfer the cookies to the buttered cookie sheets. Chill the scraps, and repeat with remaining dough.

7. Bake the cookies for 10 to 12 minutes, or until they are firm when pressed. Transfer to a rack to cool.

"Had I but a penny in the world, thou shouldst have it for gingerbread."

WILLIAM SHAKESPEARE
Love's Labour's Lost

SHORTBREAD CUTOUTS

Celestial shapes, like the sun, moon and stars, not only look but taste "out of this world." For a perfectly sweet way to express your feelings in good taste, try the Chocolate Shortbread variation, using a heart-shaped cookie cutter.

Makes 40 to 45 cookies

2 cups all-purpose flour
¼ teaspoon salt
6 ounces (1 ½ sticks) butter
½ cup granulated sugar
⅓ cup crystal sugar for garnish

1. Preheat the oven to 325° F.

2. Sift the flour and salt together.

3. Cream the butter and sugar until smooth and light. Stir in the flour until just blended. Do not overwork the dough.

4. Gather the dough into a ball and divide into halves. Roll out each half between 2 sheets of wax paper to ¼-inch thickness.

5. With 1 ½-inch cookie cutters, stamp out the cookies and transfer to an ungreased cookie sheet. Sprinkle the crystal sugar over the cookies. Repeat with remaining dough.

6. Bake the cookies for 18 to 20 minutes, or until they are firm to the touch.

7. Transfer to racks to cool.

BROWN SUGAR SHORTBREAD. In step 3, use ½ cup packed light or dark brown sugar in place of granulated sugar.

GINGER SHORTBREAD. In step 2, add 1 teaspoon ground ginger.

CARDAMOM AND NUTMEG SHORTBREAD. In step 2, add 1 teaspoon grated nutmeg and ½ teaspoon ground cardamom.

CHOCOLATE SHORTBREAD. At the end of step 2, add ½ cup Dutch-process unsweetened cocoa powder. Increase the butter to 8 ounces.

HAZELNUT SABLES

Also called Sand Cookies because of their grainy texture. Sablés have been a favorite in France for centuries.

Makes 30 to 35 cookies

1 cup ground hazelnuts
2 cups all-purpose flour
¼ teaspoon salt
⅔ cup confectioners' sugar
6 ounces (1½ sticks) butter, chilled
1 whole egg
1 egg yolk
1 teaspoon rum extract

Glaze
1 egg yolk
1 teaspoon water

Garnish
⅓ cup coarsely chopped blanched hazelnuts (see page 14 for blanching)

1. Preheat the oven to 375° F. Lightly grease cookie sheets.

2. Combine the ground hazelnuts, flour, salt and confectioners' sugar. Cut the butter into very thin slices; toss it with the flour mixture. Using your fingertips, rub the ingredients together until the mixture resembles coarse oatmeal.

3. Beat together the whole egg, egg yolk and rum extract. Pour over the dough and blend with a fork until evenly moistened.

4. Gather the dough into a ball and press to form a 5-inch disk. Wrap the dough in foil and chill for about 1 hour, or until firm.

5. With a lightly floured rolling pin, roll out the dough on a floured work surface to ¼-inch thickness. Using a 2-inch-round cookie cutter, stamp out cookies as close together as possible; transfer to the buttered cookie sheets placing 1 inch apart. Repeat the process with the scraps of remaining dough.

6. To make the glaze, beat the egg yolk and water together. Coat the cookies evenly with a pastry brush. Decorate the centers with the chopped hazelnuts.

7. Bake the cookies for 15 to 18 minutes, or until they are golden brown and firm to the touch. Transfer to racks to cool.

CINNAMON STARS

These are light-as-air, meringue-topped cookies containing no butter or flour.

Makes 55 to 60 cookies

6 egg whites
¼ teaspoon salt
2½ cups confectioners' sugar
2 teaspoons lemon zest
2 teaspoons ground cinnamon
1¼ pounds blanched ground almonds

1. Preheat the oven to 300° F.

2. With an electric mixer, beat the egg whites with the salt until soft peaks form. Gradually beat in the sugar; continue beating for about 7 minutes, or until the mixture is stiff.

3. Beat in the lemon zest and cinnamon until just blended. Reserve 1 cup of this mixture for coating the cookies before baking.

4. Fold the ground almonds into the remaining meringue mixture. Divide the dough into halves.

5. Generously cover the work surface with equal amounts of flour and confectioners' sugar. With a floured and sugared rolling pin, roll out the dough to ¼-inch thickness, using light but firm strokes. Use additional flour and sugar as needed to prevent the dough from sticking. With a 1½-inch star-shaped cookie cutter dipped into flour and sugar, cut out cookies. Transfer to an ungreased cookie sheet. Repeat the procedure with remaining dough and scraps.

6. Using a pastry brush, cover the stars with a thin layer of the reserved meringue. Bake the cookies for 20 to 22 minutes, until they feel firm and dry to the touch. Cool completely on racks.

SAY IT WITH COOKIES

What do you give to the person who has everything? Why not a basket, box, jar or tin of cookies? Fill an open-weave country basket with an unpretentious assortment of cookies, such as Oatmeal Raisin, Walnut and Date Rocks, Chocolate Chip and Peanut Butter Cookies. For Valentine's Day present your sweetie with a gold-foil-wrapped box of chocolates—Chocolate Shortbread Hearts, Fudge Brownies and Florentines. Or stick to a gift of cookies that reflect one shape; for example, round Snaps in a sugar and spice assortment. Other gift themes might be a "Celestial Selection" of shortbread suns, moons and stars; "Mixed Nuts" (cookies, of course); and cookies all of the same color (see page 93 for "Winter Whites"). The gift of cookies is always received with relish and remembered with fondness.

SUGAR COOKIES

In the eighteenth century, sugar was so highly prized and expensive that 4 loaves of sugar, weighing about 10 pounds each, were worth as much as a walnut desk.

Makes 30 to 35 cookies

4 ounces (1 stick) butter
¾ cup granulated sugar
1 egg, lightly beaten
1 tablespoon vanilla extract
1¾ cups flour
½ teaspoon salt
2 teaspoons baking powder
1 tablespoon milk
crystal or colored sugar for sprinkling

1. Preheat oven to 400° F. 15 to 30 minutes before you are ready to bake the cookies. Butter cookie sheets.

2. Cream the butter and sugar until light and fluffy. Beat in the egg until well blended; stir in the vanilla extract.

3. Sift the flour, salt and baking powder together. Add half of the dry ingredients to the creamed mixture; stir in the milk, blending well. Add remaining dry ingredients.

4. Chill the dough for about 1 hour or until firm. On a lightly floured surface, roll out the dough to ⅛-inch thickness. Using a 2½-inch cookie cutter, stamp out shapes and transfer to the buttered cookie sheets, placing them 1½ inches apart.

5. Sprinkle the cookies generously with the crystal sugar and bake for 8 to 10 minutes, or until the edges are slightly golden. Transfer to racks to cool.

"First clarify the sugar by boiling and skimming the mixture. To 3 pounds of flour, sprinkle a tea cup of fine-powdered coriander seed, rub in one pound butter, and 1½ pounds of sugar, dissolve three teaspoonfuls of pearl ash in a tea cup of milk, knead all together well, roll three-quarters of an inch thick, and cut or stamp into shape and size you please. Bake slowly fifteen or twenty minutes, tho' hard and dry at first, if put into an earthen pot, and dry cellar, or damp room, they will be finer, softer and better when six months old."

AMELIA SIMMONS, orphan
American Cookery, 1796

Drop Cookies

These are cookies with a long history and a big variety of ingredients. The dough is usually soft and the cookies spread during baking, so remember to leave a generous amount of space between the unbaked mounds of dough. To drop, use 2 teaspoons (not measuring spoons), one to pick up the dough, the other to push it onto the cookie sheet. Drop cookies are among the quickest and easiest to make. Most of these recipes provide a generous yield and are ideal for freezing.

HERMITS

The longer they sit, the better they taste. This is one cookie that improves with age.

Makes 45 to 50 cookies

2½ cups all-purpose flour
½ teaspoon baking soda
½ teaspoon salt
1 teaspoon grated nutmeg
1½ teaspoons ground cinnamon
6 ounces (1½ sticks) butter
1½ cups packed light brown sugar
2 eggs, lightly beaten
1⅓ cups chopped walnuts
1 cup dark raisins
1 cup golden raisins or currants

1. Preheat the oven to 375° F. Butter cookie sheets.

2. Sift the flour, baking soda, salt, nutmeg and cinnamon together.

3. Cream the butter and sugar until light and smooth; beat in the eggs until well blended.

4. Stir the dry ingredients into the creamed mixture until thoroughly combined; mix in the walnuts and raisins.

5. Using 2 teaspoons, drop the batter by round spoonfuls, 2 inches apart, onto the buttered cookie sheets. Bake for 10 to 12 minutes, or until the cookies are golden brown. Cool on racks.

THE ORIGINAL HERMITS

Baking cookies in the 1700s was no picnic. Original Hermits were made with almost any ingredients a practical cook could lay her hands on—always spices, sometimes molasses or maybe brown sugar, nuts and fruits. Cookies were also made in enormous batches and stored for months at a time. Life was very different then. So were cookies.

SESAME SEED WAFERS

Also called Benne Wafers, this is an early American cookie recipe which originated in South Carolina.

Makes 75 to 80 cookies

1 cup sesame seeds
6 ounces (1½ sticks) butter
1½ cups packed light brown sugar
1½ teaspoons vanilla extract
1 egg, lightly beaten
1¼ cups all-purpose flour
¼ teaspoon baking powder
¼ teaspoon salt

1. Place the sesame seeds in a baking pan and toast them in a 350° F. oven for 15 minutes, or until lightly browned. Stir occasionally.

2. Reset the oven to 275° F. Line cookie sheets with well-buttered foil.

3. In a heavy saucepan over low heat melt the butter. In a bowl, combine the melted butter and the brown sugar; stir in the vanilla extract and egg.

4. Mix the flour, baking powder and salt together; add to the butter mixture. Mix in the toasted sesame seeds and continue stirring until thoroughly combined.

5. Drop the batter by scant teaspoons, about 2½ inches apart, onto the buttered foil. Bake for 15 to 20 minutes, or until the cookies are uniformly browned; toward the end of the baking time, check often to avoid burning.

6. Remove the foil from the cookie sheets. After about 1 minute, gently peel away the cookies and cool on racks.

WALNUT JUMBLES

Many cookies of American heritage have descriptive names with obvious implications—rocks, jumbles, brambles, cracks and hermits among them. Recipes for jumbles have appeared in English cookbooks since the seventeenth century. Traditionally, they were ring-shaped cookies but can be dropped in mounds—as are these—with equal success.

Makes 45 to 50 cookies

8 ounces (2 sticks) butter
1⅓ cups packed dark brown sugar
2 eggs, lightly beaten
1 teaspoon vanilla extract
2¼ cups all-purpose flour
½ teaspoon baking soda
½ teaspoon salt
¾ cup dairy sour cream
2½ cups chopped walnuts

1. Preheat the oven to 375° F. Butter cookie sheets.

2. Cream the butter and sugar until light and smooth. Add the eggs and vanilla extract; blend well.

3. Sift the flour, baking soda and salt together. Stir the sour cream into the creamed mixture. Add the dry ingredients, beating until thoroughly combined. Stir in the walnuts. Chill for 1 hour.

4. Drop the dough by rounded tablespoons, 2½ inches apart, onto the buttered cookie sheets. Bake for 10 to 12 minutes, or until the sides of the cookies are firm to the touch. Cool on racks.

CHOCOLATE WALNUT ROCKS

Another adaptation of an American cookie classic dating back to colonial days. "Rocks" take their name not from their texture, but from their shape.

Makes 45 to 50 cookies

2 squares (2 ounces) semisweet chocolate
2 squares (2 ounces) unsweetened chocolate
⅓ cup (5 ⅓ tablespoons) butter
1 ½ cups granulated sugar
3 eggs, lightly beaten
1 teaspoon almond extract
2 cups all-purpose flour
2 teaspoons baking powder
½ teaspoon salt
1 ½ cups finely chopped walnuts
2 cups confectioners' sugar

1. Preheat the oven to 350° F.

2. In a heavy saucepan over low heat, or in the top pan of a double boiler, melt both kinds of chocolate and the butter together; cool to room temperature. Add the sugar, eggs and almond extract; stir well.

3. Mix the flour, baking powder and salt together. Add the finely chopped walnuts and combine with the chocolate mixture, blending until thoroughly incorporated. Refrigerate the dough for 1 hour.

4. Form the dough into 1-inch balls and roll in confectioners' sugar, coating the balls heavily. Arrange 2 inches apart on ungreased cookie sheets and press each ball very slightly; do not flatten.

5. Bake for 15 to 18 minutes, or until the outer part of the cookie is hard and the confectioners' sugar has a rocky, cracked look. Remove from the cookie sheets immediately. Cool on a rack.

MAPLE NUT SANDWICHES

Use pure maple syrup. The flavor is uniquely different from pancake syrup blends that contain very little maple syrup.

Makes 25 to 30 cookies

3 ounces (¾ stick) butter
1 cup pure maple syrup
¼ cup milk
2 eggs, lightly beaten
2 cups all-purpose flour
1 teaspoon baking soda
½ teaspoon salt
2 teaspoons cream of tartar
1 cup finely chopped walnuts

Brown Butter Frosting

4 ounces (1 stick) butter
2 cups confectioners' sugar
3 tablespoons maple syrup
⅛ teaspoon salt
1 tablespoon hot water

1. Preheat the oven to 400° F. Lightly butter cookie sheets.

2. In a heavy saucepan over very low heat melt the butter; mix in the maple syrup.

3. Beat the milk and eggs together; add to the syrup mixture.

4. Sift the flour, baking soda, salt and cream of tartar together; gradually add to the syrup mixture, blending well. Fold in the walnuts. Refrigerate the dough for 1 hour, or until firm.

5. Drop the dough by rounded teaspoons, 2 inches apart, onto lightly buttered cookie sheets. Bake for 8 to 10 minutes or until firm and golden brown. Cool on a rack.

6. To make the frosting, melt the butter in a heavy saucepan over very low heat, until it is lightly browned. Off the heat, add the confectioners' sugar, maple syrup, salt and hot water; stir until it becomes spreadable. When the cookies are completely cooled, frost the bottom of a cookie and gently press to the bottom of a plain cookie to make a sandwich.

BUTTERSCOTCH DROPS

Makes 35 to 40 cookies

4 ounces (1 stick) butter
1 ¼ cups packed dark brown sugar
1 egg, lightly beaten
¼ cup water
1 teaspoon vanilla extract
1 ¾ cups all-purpose flour
½ teaspoon baking soda
¼ teaspoon salt
½ cup finely chopped pecans or walnuts

1. Preheat the oven to 400° F. Lightly butter cookie sheets.

2. Combine the butter and brown sugar until smooth. Add the egg; stir in the water and vanilla extract and continue mixing until completely combined.

3. Sift the flour, baking soda and salt together; stir into the creamed mixture until the flour mixture is thoroughly incorporated. Chill the dough for 15 minutes.

4. Using a teaspoon, scoop up well-rounded spoons of dough and gently press the tops into the chopped nuts, being careful not to flatten the mounds. Using another teaspoon, gently push the dough, with the nuts on top, onto the buttered cookie sheets, placing the mounds about 2 ½ inches apart. Bake for 8 to 10 minutes, or until the cookies are just firm. Cool on racks.

MELTING MOLASSES DROPS

Makes 35 to 40 cookies

2 cups all-purpose flour
1 teaspoon baking soda
½ teaspoon salt
1 teaspoon ground cinnamon
½ teaspoon grated nutmeg
¼ teaspoon ground allspice
¼ teaspoon ground ginger
¾ cup packed dark brown sugar
6 ounces (1½ sticks) butter
1 egg, lightly beaten
⅓ cup dark molasses
1 teaspoon vanilla extract

1. Preheat the oven to 350° F. Butter the cookie sheets.

2. Sift the flour, baking soda, salt, cinnamon, nutmeg, allspice and ginger together.

3. Cream the brown sugar and butter until light and fluffy. Beat in the egg and combine thoroughly. Mix in the molasses and vanilla extract; add the flour mixture and stir until all the ingredients are thoroughly blended.

4. Using 2 tablespoons, drop dough by level spoonfuls 3 inches apart onto the buttered cookie sheets. Bake for 12 to 14 minutes, or until the edges of the cookies are browned but still slightly soft in the center. Wait about 30 seconds before removing the cookies from the cookie sheet. Cool on a rack.

MOLASSES NUT DROPS. Add 1 cup finely chopped pecans or walnuts at the end of step 3.

PECAN LACE CURLS

Makes 35 to 40 cookies

1 cup all-purpose flour
1⅓ cups finely chopped pecans
4 ounces (1 stick) butter
½ cup packed light brown sugar
¼ cup dark corn syrup
¼ cup light corn syrup
1 teaspoon vanilla extract

1. Preheat the oven to 325° F. Lightly butter cookie sheets.

2. Sift the flour; combine with the chopped pecans.

3. In a heavy saucepan over low heat, melt the butter, brown sugar and both kinds of corn syrup together. Remove from heat and gradually add the flour mixture. Stir in the vanilla. Drop by level teaspoons 3 inches apart onto the buttered cookie sheets. Bake for 8 to 10 minutes, or until cookies are caramel color.

4. Cool for 1 minute on the cookie sheet, or until a wide metal spatula slips under the cookie without breaking off the edges. While warm, roll each cookie around the handle of a wooden spoon. Place the curls on racks to cool completely. If the cookies harden too quickly, return the cookie sheet to the oven for 1 minute to soften the cookies before attempting to remove and roll.

COCONUT MACAROONS

This type of macaroon has a golden-colored outside shell and a soft, sweet center.

Makes 20 to 25 cookies

2 cups shredded coconut
⅔ cup sweetened condensed milk
2 tablespoons heavy cream
1 ½ teaspoons vanilla extract
⅓ cup all-purpose flour
pinch of salt

1. Preheat the oven to 300° F. Butter cookie sheets.

2. Mix the coconut, condensed milk, heavy cream and vanilla extract together in a small bowl.

3. Combine the flour and salt; add to the coconut mixture and stir until flour mixture is incorporated. The batter will be thick and moist.

4. Using a 1-tablespoon measuring spoon, drop the batter onto the buttered cookie sheet, leaving 2 inches between the mounds. Bake for 15 to 18 minutes, or just until cookies are a toasty golden brown.

5. Immediately transfer the cookies to a rack to cool.

CHOCOLATE CHIP COCONUT MACA-ROONS. In step 3, add ½ cup (3 ounces) miniature semisweet chocolate chips, or regular-size chocolate chips that have been coarsely chopped.

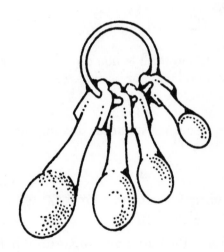

CRISPY LEMON OR ORANGE ZEST WAFERS

Use only fresh lemon or orange zest. The processed, dried version does not impart the same tart citrus flavor to these delicate wafer cookies.

Makes 45 to 50 cookies

6 ounces (1½ sticks) butter
1 cup granulated sugar
1 egg
1 tablespoon fresh lemon or orange juice
1 teaspoon lemon or orange zest (see page 15)
1 cup all-purpose flour
lemon or orange sugar for dusting (see page 16)

1. Preheat the oven to 375° F. Generously butter cookie sheets.

2. Cream the butter and sugar until light and fluffy. Add the egg, lemon or orange juice and zest and continue beating until smooth.

3. Sift the flour; gradually add to the creamed mixture, stirring until thoroughly combined.

4. Using 2 teaspoons, drop the dough 2 inches apart onto the buttered cookie sheets. Bake for 8 to 10 minutes, or until edges are golden brown.

5. Wait for 30 seconds before removing the cookies with a wide metal spatula to cool on racks. As the cookies cool, they will become very crisp. Lightly dust the cookies with lemon or orange sugar.

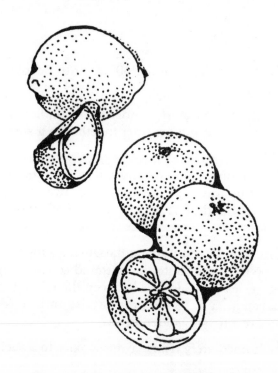

WALNUT AND DATE ROCKS

Hermits, Brambles, Crinkles, Snickerdoodles and Rocks have been made in the kitchens of America since the early days. These cookies use very basic ingredients including brown sugar, which was much less expensive than white sugar in the eighteenth and nineteenth centuries.

Makes 45 to 50 cookies

14 ounces (3½ sticks) butter
¾ cup packed light brown sugar
¾ cup packed dark brown sugar
3 eggs, separated
1 teaspoon vanilla extract
4 cups all-purpose flour
1 teaspoon baking soda
¼ teaspoon salt
1 teaspoon ground allspice
1 tablespoon ground cinnamon
1½ cups chopped pitted dates
1½ cups very coarsely chopped walnuts
confectioners' sugar or superfine sugar for
      garnish

1. Preheat the oven to 375° F. Butter cookie sheets.

2. Cream the butter and both kinds of brown sugar together; add the egg yolks and vanilla extract.

3. Sift the flour, baking soda, salt, allspice and cinnamon together. Add to the creamed mixture, beating until thoroughly combined.

4. With an electric mixer or wire whisk, beat the egg whites until foamy; add to batter, stirring until completely incorporated. Blend in the dates and walnuts.

5. Using 2 teaspoons, drop the batter by rounded spoonfuls onto the buttered cookie sheets, leaving 2 inches between the nuggets of batter. Bake for 15 to 16 minutes, or just until done in the center.

6. Remove to a rack to cool. While the cookies are still warm, sprinkle them with confectioners' sugar through a strainer or with superfine sugar.

ANISE DROPS

These pale yellow rounds form their own crackly white frosting crown while they bake. They must set out overnight to dry before baking, so you must plan to make these delightful anise cookies. Anise Drops are traditionally made in Bavaria at Christmastime.

Makes 45 to 50 cookies

1 ¾ cups all-purpose flour
½ teaspoon baking powder
½ teaspoon salt
3 eggs
1 cup plus 2 tablespoons superfine sugar
2 teaspoons pure anise extract

1. Preheat the oven to 325° F. 15 to 30 minutes before you are ready to bake the cookies. Generously butter cookie sheets.

2. Sift the flour, baking powder and salt together. Set aside.

3. Using an electric mixer set at medium speed, beat the eggs until light and fluffy. While beating, gradually add the sugar and continue to beat for 10 minutes.

4. Adjust mixer speed to low and add the dry ingredients; blend in the anise extract.

5. Using 2 teaspoons, drop the batter by rounded spoonfuls about ½ inch apart onto the buttered cookie sheets. With the back of a spoon, swirl the dough to make flat rounds. Allow the cookies to stand out overnight, or for at least 8 hours, to dry.

6. Bake for 8 to 10 minutes, or until the tops have turned a creamy golden color but cookies are not brown on the tops or bottoms. Cool the cookies on racks.

BUTTER WAFERS

The butter wafer is an especially fragile cookie—brown-edged and very crispy. For variety, divide the basic recipe into halves and select several flavor variations that follow.

Makes 45 to 50 cookies

8 ounces (2 sticks) butter
⅔ cup granulated sugar
1 teaspoon vanilla extract
2 eggs
⅔ cup all-purpose flour
vanilla, cocoa, butter rum or cardamom
    flavoring (see variations)

1. Preheat the oven to 350° F. Lightly butter cookie sheets.

2. Cream the butter. When it is soft and fluffy, add the sugar and continue beating for about 3 minutes, or until very light; beat in the vanilla extract. Add the eggs and continue beating until all the ingredients are combined.

3. Sift the flour; combine with the creamed mixture, beating only until the ingredients are blended.

4. Using 2 teaspoons, drop the batter by level spoonfuls about 3½ inches apart onto the buttered cookie sheets.

5. Bake for 15 to 18 minutes, or until the edges are well browned. Immediately remove the cookies to racks to cool.

VANILLA BUTTER WAFERS. Increase vanilla extract by 1 teaspoon.

COCOA WAFERS. In step 3, sift ¼ cup unsweetened Dutch-process cocoa powder along with the flour.

BUTTER RUM WAFERS. In place of vanilla extract, add 2 teaspoons pure rum extract.

CARDAMOM BUTTER WAFERS. Omit vanilla extract. Add 1 teaspoon ground cardamom and 1 teaspoon grated orange zest after the flour in step 3.

CRISPY OATMEAL THINS

These are wafer-type cookies with a lacy texture. Make them large or small. One tablespoon of dough yields a large cookie; 1 teaspoon of dough yields a small cookie.

Makes 35 to 40 cookies

8 ounces (2 sticks) butter
½ cup granulated sugar
1 cup packed light brown sugar
2 eggs, lightly beaten
2 teaspoons vanilla extract
¼ cup water
1 cup all-purpose flour
¼ teaspoon salt
½ teaspoon baking soda
2 cups quick-cooking (*not* instant) oatmeal
1½ cups finely chopped walnuts

1. Preheat the oven to 350° F. Butter cookie sheets.

2. Cream the butter and both kinds of sugar together until light and fluffy. Add the eggs, vanilla extract and water; continue beating until well combined.

3. Sift the flour, salt and baking soda together. Gradually add the dry ingredients to the creamed mixture, beating until smooth. Stir in the oatmeal and walnuts.

4. Using 2 tablespoons, drop the dough by rounded spoonfuls about 4 inches apart onto the buttered cookie sheets. These cookies spread quite a bit while baking, so leave plenty of room between the mounds of batter. Spread the cookies to about ¼-inch thickness with the back of a spoon. Bake for 8 to 10 minutes, or until the cookies are golden brown.

5. Cool on the cookie sheet for 1 minute. Using a wide metal spatula, remove the cookies to racks to cool.

CHEWY OATMEAL COOKIES

Makes 45 to 50 cookies

6 ounces (1½ sticks) butter
1⅓ cups packed dark brown sugar
2 eggs, lightly beaten
1 teaspoon vanilla extract
1 cup all-purpose flour
¼ teaspoon baking soda
1 teaspoon salt
1 teaspoon ground cinnamon
3½ cups quick-cooking (*not* instant) oats
2 tablespoons water

1. Preheat the oven to 350° F. Butter cookie sheets.

2. In a large mixing bowl, cream together the butter and brown sugar. Beat in the eggs and vanilla.

3. Combine the flour, baking soda, salt, cinnamon and oats.

4. Add the dry ingredients to the butter mixture and combine thoroughly. Blend in the water.

5. Using 2 tablespoons, drop the cookies by rounded spoonfuls 2 inches apart onto the buttered cookie sheets.

6. Bake for 12 to 14 minutes, or until the cookies are light brown on the bottom.

7. Remove the cookies from the oven and wait a few seconds before placing them on racks to cool.

RAISIN SPICE. In step 3, add ¼ teaspoon ground allspice to the dry ingredients and increase cinnamon by ½ teaspoon. Add 1 cup dark raisins at the end of step 4. Bake as directed.

DATE NUT. At the end of step 4, add ½ cup pitted, chopped dates and ½ cup slivered almonds. Bake as directed.

CURRANT OATMEAL. At the end of step 4, add 1½ cups dried currants.

RUM WALNUT. At the end of step 4, omit the water and add 2 tablespoons dark rum and 1 cup coarsely chopped walnuts.

CASHEW DROPS

This soft, cakelike cookie contains whole toasted cashews, which have an especially intense flavor and wonderfully crunchy texture. Buy raw, unsalted cashews and toast in a 350° F. oven for 10 to 15 minutes, or until golden brown.

Makes 35 to 40 cookies

4 ounces (1 stick) butter
1 cup packed light brown sugar
1 egg
1 teaspoon vanilla extract
1 cup all-purpose flour
¾ teaspoon baking soda
¾ teaspoon baking powder
¼ teaspoon salt
⅓ cup dairy sour cream
2 cups toasted whole cashews

1. Preheat the oven to 400° F. Butter cookie sheets.

2. Cream the butter and brown sugar until light and fluffy. Add the egg and vanilla; mix thoroughly.

3. Sift the flour, baking soda, baking powder and salt together. Add half of the sour cream and half of the flour mixture to the creamed mixture, blending well. Repeat with remaining flour mixture and sour cream.

4. Fold in the toasted cashews. Drop the batter by teaspoons 1½ inches apart onto the buttered cookie sheets.

5. Bake for 8 to 10 minutes, or until cookies are a light golden brown. Cool on racks.

ALMOND CRUNCH COOKIES

This big crunchy cookie is absolutely stuffed with almond pieces. A true "milk and cookies" cookie.

Makes 35 to 40 cookies

2 ¼ cups all-purpose flour
½ teaspoon salt
½ teaspoon baking soda
1 teaspoon ground cinnamon
½ teaspoon ground allspice
¼ teaspoon grated nutmeg
6 ounces (1 ½ sticks) butter
1 ½ cups packed dark brown sugar
2 eggs, lightly beaten
1 ½ teaspoons vanilla extract
2 cups sliced blanched almonds

1. Preheat the oven to 375° F. Butter cookie sheets.

2. Sift the flour, salt, baking soda, cinnamon, allspice and nutmeg together. Set aside.

3. Cream the butter and brown sugar until light and smooth. Beat in the eggs and vanilla extract until well blended. Add the dry ingredients and mix until thoroughly combined. Stir in the almonds.

4. Using 2 tablespoons, drop the batter by heaping spoonfuls 1 ½ inches apart onto buttered cookie sheets. Bake for 14 to 16 minutes, or until the cookies feel firm to the touch. Cool on racks.

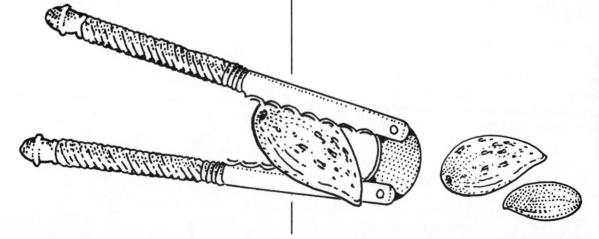

FRUITCAKE DROPS

These festively frosted and decorated cookies taste just like fruitcake, but there's no need to store them in a brandy-soaked cloth for months before serving. They're ready to eat right from the oven.

Makes 45 to 50 cookies

3 ounces (¾ stick) butter
½ cup packed light brown sugar
1 egg
¼ cup sherry, port, brandy or rum
1½ cups plus 2 tablespoons all-purpose flour
1 teaspoon baking soda
¼ teaspoon salt
¼ teaspoon grated nutmeg
⅛ teaspoon ground allspice
1 cup chopped dates
½ cup golden raisins
½ cup dried currants
1 slice of candied pineapple, chopped
½ cup chopped candied orange peel
½ cup chopped candied cherries
1½ cups coarsely chopped pecans
glaze (see Glazed Pfeffernuesse, page 106)
various fruits, nuts, candied peels, nut halves
      or candied fruits for decoration

1. Preheat the oven to 300° F. Butter cookie sheets.

2. Cream the butter and brown sugar until smooth and light. Beat in the egg; stir in the wine or liquor.

3. Sift together the flour, baking soda, salt, nutmeg and allspice; add to the creamed mixture, beating until thoroughly combined. Stir in all the fruits and the pecans.

4. Drop by rounded tablespoons 1½ inches apart onto the buttered cookie sheets.

5. Bake for 18 to 20 minutes, or until the cookies are firm to the touch. Transfer the cookies to racks to cool completely.

6. Prepare the glaze (see page 106). With a teaspoon, drizzle the glaze onto the cookies. Decorate with candied fruits or nut halves. Allow the glaze to harden before storing the cookies.

NEAPOLITAN JUMBLES

Although jumbles were typically a ring-shaped cookie back in the 1600s, this version, with its contrasting batters baked side-by-side, creates another interesting design.

Makes 40 to 45 cookies

2 squares (2 ounces) unsweetened chocolate
6 ounces (1½ sticks) butter
1 cup granulated sugar
¾ cup packed dark brown sugar
2 eggs
2 teaspoons vanilla extract
1 cup dairy sour cream
2⅔ cups all-purpose flour
½ teaspoon baking soda
¾ teaspoon salt
walnut or pecan halves or candied cherry
        halves for garnish

1. Preheat the oven to 375° F. Butter cookie sheets.

2. In a heavy saucepan over low heat or in the top pan of a double boiler, melt the chocolate. Cool to room temperature.

3. Cream the butter and both kinds of sugar until light and smooth. Beat in the eggs until well blended. Stir in the vanilla extract and the sour cream.

4. Sift the flour, baking soda and salt together. Beat into the creamed mixture until all the ingredients are thoroughly combined. Divide the mixture into halves. Add the cooled, melted chocolate to one portion and blend well.

5. Using 2 teaspoons, drop the plain batter by rounded teaspoons 3 inches apart onto the buttered cookie sheets. Then drop a rounded teaspoon of the chocolate batter next to each plain mound so the batters are touching. Press a nut or cherry half in the center of each cookie.

6. Bake for 10 to 12 minutes, or until the cookies are firm to the touch. Cool on racks.

CANDIED FRUIT

A word about candied fruit: It is best to store candied fruit at room temperature in an airtight container. Although we tend to have a passion for placing everything in the refrigerator to ensure freshness, control your passion in this case; candied fruit will crystallize and become unusable. There is a tremendous variety of candied and glazed fruit (for decorating), available at culinary specialty shops, which is supple, moist and flavorful, and does not resemble the stuff called "candied fruit" which appears on supermarket shelves once a year. (See the Mail-Order Guide on page 119 for stores that sell the real thing.)

Molded, Pressed and Hand-Formed Cookies

A clever monk, seeing a way to coax his class of schoolchildren into memorizing their daily prayers, sweetened scraps of bread dough, twisted them into the shape of children with arms folded in prayer, and handed them out to his best students. He named the thing *pretiora,* or little reward. Not long after, the sweet treats were renamed "pretzels" by Austrian bakers. They became the first of many hand-formed delights.

PECAN PUFFS

Puffs, sometimes called cacoons in nineteenth-century Southern cookbooks, are fragile cookies. Pop them into your mouth all at once, or the consequences will be very "crumby"!

Makes 35 to 40 cookies

4 ounces (1 stick) butter
½ cup granulated sugar
1 egg yolk
1 teaspoon vanilla extract
1 cup all-purpose flour
1¼ cups ground pecans
1 cup confectioners' sugar
½ teaspoon ground cinnamon
¼ teaspoon grated nutmeg

1. Preheat the oven to 300° F. Butter cookie sheets.

2. Cream the butter and granulated sugar until light and fluffy. Blend in the egg yolk; stir in the vanilla extract.

3. Sift the flour twice; blend into the creamed mixture. Stir in the pecans.

4. Chill the mixture for 15 minutes. Roll the dough into 1-inch balls and place them 1 inch apart on the buttered cookie sheets. Bake the cookies for 25 to 30 minutes, or until firm.

5. Cool cookies on the baking sheets for 1 minute before carefully transferring them to racks to cool.

6. Mix the confectioners' sugar, cinnamon and nutmeg together. Roll the cookies in the sugar mixture until well coated.

CHOCOLATE PUFFS. In a saucepan over low heat, or in the top pan of a double boiler, melt 2 squares (2 ounces) semisweet chocolate. Cool completely. Add to the creamed mixture at the end of step 2. Omit the cinnamon and nutmeg. Add 2 teaspoons of Dutch-process cocoa to the confectioners' sugar before rolling the puffs in the sugar mixture.

ALMOND PRETZELS

Makes 30 to 35 cookies

4 ounces (1 stick) butter
¾ cup confectioners' sugar
½ cup almond paste
1 egg yolk
1 whole egg
½ teaspoon vanilla extract
1½ cups all-purpose flour
1 egg white, lightly beaten, for glazing
½ cup crystal sugar for decoration

1. Preheat the oven to 375° F. 15 to 30 minutes before you are ready to bake the cookies. Butter cookie sheets.

2. Using an electric mixer, cream the butter and confectioners' sugar together until light and fluffy. Beat in the almond paste until well blended.

3. Mix in the egg yolk, the whole egg and the vanilla extract; beat in the flour until thoroughly incorporated.

4. Chill the dough for 4 to 6 hours, or until very firm.

5. Pinch off pieces of dough about the size of a walnut. On a very lightly floured surface, press and roll the dough into 8-inch "ropes" about ¼-inch thick. Form the dough into pretzel shapes. Glaze the top of each pretzel with the beaten egg white and sprinkle generously with the crystal sugar.

6. Bake the pretzels for 8 to 10 minutes, or until they start to turn golden. Cool on racks.

CHOCOLATE GLAZED PRETZELS.
Omit the egg white glaze and sugar crystals in step 5. Bake as directed. In a heavy saucepan over low heat, or in the top pan of a double boiler, melt 8 squares (8 ounces) semisweet chocolate; cool slightly. After the pretzels have cooled completely, dip them into the chocolate; place on wax paper and sprinkle with sugar crystals. Allow them to set for 1 hour.

VIENNESE CRESCENTS

Makes 45 to 50 cookies

8 ounces (2 sticks) butter
½ cup granulated sugar
1 ½ cups ground blanched almonds
2 cups all-purpose flour
½ teaspoon salt
vanilla confectioners' sugar (see page 16)

1. Preheat the oven to 350° F. 15 to 30 minutes before you are ready to bake the cookies.

2. Cream the butter and sugar until the mixture is light and fluffy. Stir in the almonds and blend well.

3. Sift the flour with the salt; stir into the creamed mixture until incorporated. Chill the dough for about 30 minutes or until firm.

4. Pinch off pieces of dough the size of large walnuts and press and roll the dough between your fingers to form crescent shapes. Place the crescents on ungreased cookie sheets and bake for 14 to 16 minutes, or until cookies are firm and the bottoms just begin to turn golden.

5. Carefully transfer the cookies to racks; while still warm, roll in vanilla confectioners' sugar.

WINTER WHITES

Create a Cookie Collection. Cookies, colors and containers. Push them to their maximum potential by creating a collection that reflects the season. For instance, "Winter Whites." Bake an attractive assortment of several different kinds of cookies, all white in color, each a distinctly different shape, texture and taste. Layer the cookies in a crystal-clear tall glass jar for the ultimate visual experience. They'll be as lovely as new fallen snow.

Recipes for the Winter White collection might include: Glazed Pfeffernuesse; Mexican Wedding Cakes; Viennese Crescents; Kourambiedes; Almond Pretzels; Linzer Cookies; Meringue Kisses and Pecan Puffs (see Index for pages).

HOLIDAY RUSKS

A rusk is a fairly plain, moderately sweet cookie that is sliced after baking and then baked a second time until it is crisp and golden. This version, with loads of crunchy almonds, becomes even more festive with the addition of green and red candied cherries.

Makes 32 cookies

3 ounces (¾ stick) butter
⅔ cup granulated sugar
2 eggs, lightly beaten
½ teaspoon almond extract
1 teaspoon rum extract
1⅔ cups all-purpose flour
1½ teaspoons baking powder
½ teaspoon salt
⅓ cup chopped green candied cherries
⅓ cup chopped red candied cherries
⅔ cup coarsely chopped blanched almonds
32 whole blanched almonds

1. Preheat the oven to 375° F. Butter and flour cookie sheets.

2. Cream the butter and sugar together until light and fluffy. Beat in the eggs until well blended; stir in the almond and rum extracts.

3. Sift together the flour, baking powder and salt. Stir the dry ingredients into the creamed mixture until thoroughly combined; fold in the red and green cherries and chopped almonds.

4. Divide the batter into 4 equal parts. Shape the dough into 2½ - x 4½-inch loaves on the buttered cookie sheets. Place 8 whole almonds lengthwise down the center of each loaf.

5. Bake for 20 minutes, or until the tops are golden. Transfer the rusks to a cutting board. Using a knife with a serrated edge, cut into ¾-inch-thick slices. Turn the oven to off; dry out the rusks in the oven for 12 to 15 minutes, turning them after 5 minutes. Cool completely on racks.

FLORENTINES

Store these fragile, candylike holiday cookies between sheets of wax paper in covered tins. Do not refrigerate or the chocolate will turn cloudy and the candied fruit will crystallize.

Makes 25 to 30 cookies

3 tablespoons butter
½ cup heavy cream
⅓ cup granulated sugar
¾ cup chopped candied orange peel
¼ cup chopped candied red cherries
1 cup sliced blanched almonds
¼ cup all-purpose flour
8 squares (8 ounces) semisweet chocolate

1. Preheat the oven to 375° F. Butter cookie sheets.

2. In a small heavy saucepan combine the butter, cream and sugar. Bring the mixture to a boil over low heat.

3. Stir in the candied orange peel, candied cherries, almonds and flour.

4. Drop the batter by level tablespoons about 3 inches apart onto the buttered cookie sheets. Flatten each cookie with a fork dipped into cold water to form 2-inch rounds.

5. Bake the cookies for 10 to 12 minutes or until golden brown. Allow the cookies to set for 1 minute on the sheets before removing. Using a wide metal spatula, transfer the cookies to racks to cool completely.

6. In a small heavy saucepan over low heat, or in the top pan of a double boiler, melt the chocolate. Cool slightly. Brush the underside of the florentines with a thin layer of the melted chocolate. Using a decorating comb or a fork, gently make a wavy line pattern on the chocolate. With the chocolate side up transfer the cookies to a sheet of wax paper to set for 1 hour.

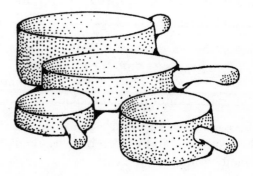

PEANUT BUTTER COOKIES

Makes 50 to 55 cookies

4 ounces (1 stick) butter
½ cup chunky peanut butter
½ cup packed light brown sugar
½ cup granulated sugar
1 egg, lightly beaten
1 teaspoon vanilla extract
1 ¾ cups all-purpose flour
½ teaspoon baking soda
¼ teaspoon salt

1. Preheat the oven to 375° F.

2. Cream the butter, peanut butter and both kinds of sugar together until smooth. Stir in the egg and vanilla extract; blend well.

3. Mix the flour, baking soda and salt together; add to the creamed mixture until thoroughly combined.

4. Spoon the batter by rounded teaspoons about 2 inches apart onto the ungreased cookie sheets. With a fork, press a crosshatch design in the center of each cookie.

5. Bake for 10 to 12 minutes, or until the cookies are firm and golden brown. Cool completely on racks.

PEANUT BUTTER NUT COOKIES. Add 1 cup unsalted, roasted peanuts to the batter at the end of step 3.

PEANUT BUTTER RAISIN DROPS. Add 1 cup dark raisins to the batter at the end of step 3.

PEANUT BUTTER CHOCOLATE CHIP COOKIES. Add 1 cup (6 ounces) semisweet chocolate chips to the batter at the end of step 3.

PEANUT BUTTER KISSES. Shape the dough into 1 ½-inch balls. Roll in superfine sugar and place on ungreased cookie sheets. Bake as directed. Remove the cookies from the oven and, while still on the cookie sheet, immediately press a chocolate kiss into the center. Cool on racks.

PEANUT BUTTER AND JELLY CUPS. Shape the dough into 1 ½-inch balls. Bake as directed. Remove from the oven and while still warm, press the center of each cookie with the back of a teaspoon to form a cup. Fill the cup with ½ teaspoon of the jam or preserves of your choice. Cool on racks.

CASHEW NUT BUTTER COOKIES. In place of peanut butter in step 2, substitute ½ cup cashew butter (available in health-food stores).

ALMOND NUT BUTTER COOKIES. In place of peanut butter, in step 2, substitute ½ cup almond butter (available in health-food stores).

GIANT PEANUT BUTTER COOKIES. To make giant Peanut Butter Cookies, measure ¼ cup dough per cookie. Place the mounds of dough 5 inches apart on the cookie sheet. With a rubber spatula flatten each cookie to 4 inches in diameter and make a crosshatch design. Bake for 12 to 14 minutes.

MINIATURE CHOCOLATE CRACKS

Makes 35 to 40 cookies

6 squares (6 ounces) semisweet chocolate
2 squares (2 ounces) unsweetened chocolate
2 tablespoons (¼ stick) butter
4 egg yolks
½ cup packed dark brown sugar
1½ teaspoons rum extract
2 cups finely chopped blanched hazelnuts
    (see page 14)
¾ cup all-purpose flour
⅓ cup dark brown sugar, sifted twice

1. Preheat the oven to 350° F. Butter cookie sheets.

2. In a heavy saucepan over very low heat, or in the top pan of a double boiler, melt both kinds of chocolate and butter together. Cool to room temperature.

3. Beat the egg yolks and ½ cup sugar together until the mixture is thick and falls into a ribbon. Stir in the melted chocolate and butter mixture until well blended; add in the rum extract and hazelnuts.

4. Add the flour, stirring until thoroughly incorporated.

5. Form the dough into 1-inch balls and place them on the buttered cookie sheets. Bake for 10 to 12 minutes, or until the cookies are crackled on top and feel firm to the touch. Remove to a bowl containing the brown sugar; coat completely. Transfer the cookies to racks to cool.

PECAN TARTLETS

The taste is reminiscent of a pecan pie. The macadamia nut variation calls for *unsalted* nuts, often found in culinary specialty stores (Mail-Order Guide, see page 119).

Makes 48 tartlets

Pastry
6 ounces (1 ½ sticks) butter
⅓ cup granulated sugar
2 cups all-purpose flour
¼ teaspoon salt

Filling
3 ounces (¾ stick) butter
⅔ cup sugar
3 eggs, lightly beaten
½ teaspoon salt
½ cup dark corn syrup
1 teaspoon vanilla extract
1 ⅓ cups finely chopped pecans
48 pecan halves for decoration

1. Preheat the oven to 400° F. 15 to 30 minutes before you are ready to bake the tartlets.

2. To prepare the pastry, cream together the butter and sugar until smooth.

3. Sift the flour and salt together; stir into the creamed mixture and blend well.

4. Pinch off pieces of dough to make ½-inch balls. Press a ball of the dough into each minimuffin tin mold to a thickness of about ⅛ inch. Chill for 15 minutes.

5. To prepare the filling, cream the butter and sugar until well blended. Beat in the eggs; add the salt, corn syrup and vanilla. Blend well, stir in the chopped pecans.

6. Spoon the mixture into the pastry, using about 1 tablespoon for each tartlet cup. The filling and pastry should be level at the rims. Decorate each with a pecan half.

7. Place the muffin tins on a cookie sheet and bake for 25 minutes, or until the pastry is a rich golden brown.

8. Cool the pans on a rack for 5 minutes. While the cookies are still warm, twist each gently to loosen from the pan. Remove the tartlets from the pan and cool on racks.

MACADAMIA NUT TARTLETS. Omit the pecans and use 1 ⅓ cups finely chopped macadamia nuts. Decorate each tartlet with a macadamia nut half.

MINIMUFFIN TINS

You will need at least one minimuffin tin which has 12 molds, each measuring ¾ inch deep and 1 ¾ inches across the top. They need not be greased since this pastry dough contains a large amount of butter—enough to prevent the individual tartlets from sticking. Once you become familiar with the simple procedure of making tartlets, put your pan to good use and try making Brownie Cups (see page 34).

LINZER CUPS

Makes 20 to 25 cookies

1 cup all-purpose flour
2 teaspoons Dutch-process cocoa
½ teaspoon ground cinnamon
¼ teaspoon ground cloves
¼ teaspoon salt
4 ounces (1 stick) butter
½ cup granulated sugar
1 egg yolk
1 teaspoon vanilla extract
½ teaspoon grated lemon zest
½ cup ground hazelnuts
½ to ¾ cup red raspberry, apricot or currant jam

1. Preheat the oven to 350° F. 15 to 30 minutes before you are ready to bake the cookies. Butter cookie sheets.

2. Sift together the flour, cocoa, cinnamon, cloves and salt.

3. Cream together the butter and sugar until light and fluffy; blend in the egg yolk. Stir in the vanilla extract, lemon zest and ground hazelnuts.

4. Beat the dry ingredients into the creamed mixture until thoroughly combined.

5. Chill the dough for about 3 hours, or until very firm.

6. Roll the dough into 1-inch balls. Using the back of a teaspoon, make an indentation in the center of each ball about ½ inch deep. Place the cookies on the buttered cookie sheets.

7. Bake for 8 to 10 minutes, or until the cookies feel firm to the touch. Cool on racks. When the cookies are completely cool, fill the centers with a rounded teaspoon of jam.

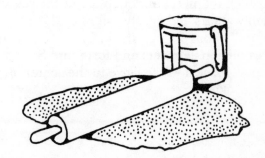

KOURAMBIEDES

Makes 80 to 85 cookies

1 pound (4 sticks) butter
½ cup granulated sugar
1 egg yolk
2 tablespoons brandy
4 cups all-purpose flour, sifted
whole cloves, about 80
2 cups confectioners' sugar

1. Preheat the oven to 350° F.

2. Cream the butter until smooth and almost white, 10 to 15 minutes with an electric mixer.

3. Blend in the granulated sugar until thoroughly combined; stir in the egg yolk and then the brandy. Beat in the flour until competely incorporated.

4. Pinch off pieces of dough about the size of small walnuts and gently roll into 2½-inch "ropes" about ⅜ inch thick. Place 1½ inches apart on cookie sheets and form into S shapes. Place a whole clove in the center of each cookie.

5. Bake the cookies for 15 to 18 minutes, or until firm to the touch and barely golden. Wait a few seconds and with a wide metal spatula carefully transfer the cookies to racks set on top of a sheet of wax paper. Sift a thick layer of confectioners' sugar over the tops of the cookies.

LEGENDARY GREEK BUTTER COOKIES

There are countless family recipes for the light, fragrant Christmas shortbread made in Greece. It is a cookie of ancient origins. The supposed secret of Kourambiedes is said to lie in beating the butter and sugar by hand for at least 30 minutes, but an electric mixer can be used with perfect results.

MEXICAN WEDDING CAKES

Makes 35 to 40 cookies

8 ounces (2 sticks) butter
⅔ cup confectioners' sugar
1 teaspoon vanilla extract
2 cups all-purpose flour
1 cup finely chopped pecans
2 cups confectioners' sugar

1. Preheat the oven to 325° F. 15 to 30 minutes before you are ready to bake the cookies.

2. Cream the butter until smooth and pale yellow in color. Beat in ⅔ cup sugar until well blended; stir in the vanilla extract.

3. Mix in the flour, stirring until thoroughly blended; stir in the pecans.

4. Chill the dough for about 30 minutes, or until firm.

5. Shape the dough into 1½-inch balls. Place them 1½ inches apart on ungreased cookie sheets. Flatten them into ½-inch-thick disks.

6. Bake for 20 to 22 minutes, or until they are firm to the touch.

7. Place 2 cups confectioners' sugar in a bowl. Dip the cookies, a few at a time, into the sugar. Place on racks. When the cookies are completely cool, dip them again into the confectioners' sugar.

APRICOT ENVELOPES

Makes 35 to 40 cookies

1 ⅔ cups all-purpose flour
½ cup granulated sugar
¼ teaspoon salt
4 ounces (1 stick) butter, chilled
2 egg yolks
½ cup dairy sour cream
½ cup apricot jam

1. Preheat the oven to 350° F. 15 to 30 minutes before you are ready to bake the cookies. Butter cookie sheets.

2. Combine the flour, sugar and salt. Cut the butter into small pieces and toss into the flour mixture. Using 2 knives or a pastry blender, cut in the butter until the mixture resembles coarse oatmeal. Combine the egg yolks and sour cream; stir into the flour mixture. Chill the dough for 6 to 8 hours or overnight.

3. Divide the dough into 4 parts. On a lightly floured surface, roll out each part into a 6-inch square using additional flour only when necessary to prevent the dough from sticking. Trim the edges evenly. With a sharp knife cut the dough into 2-inch squares. Place ½ teaspoon of apricot jam in the center of each square. Using a knife, fold two opposite corners of the dough over each other, enclosing the jam.

4. Bake the cookies for 10 to 12 minutes, or until the bottoms are lightly browned. Cool on racks.

CLASSIC SHORTBREAD WEDGES

One of the richest, most buttery cookies on earth. Shortbread comes to us from Scotland, where they eat it year-round, although it makes a wonderful gift to give at Christmas.

Makes 30 to 32 cookies

2 cups all-purpose flour
¼ teaspoon salt
¼ teaspoon baking powder
8 ounces (2 sticks) butter
⅔ cup confectioners' sugar
½ teaspoon vanilla extract

1. Preheat the oven to 325° F. 15 to 30 minutes before you are ready to bake the cookies.

2. Sift the flour, salt and baking powder together three times.

3. Cream the butter until soft and smooth. Beat in the confectioners' sugar and blend well; stir in the vanilla extract. Stir in the flour mixture and combine thoroughly.

4. Scrape the dough into a ball; transfer to a sheet of aluminum foil and wrap loosely. Lightly press the dough with the palm of your hand to 1-inch thickness. Chill for 3 hours, or until firm.

5. Remove the dough from the refrigerator and let it stand at room temperature for 15 minutes. Divide into 4 equal parts.

6. On a lightly floured surface, use a floured rolling pin to roll the dough into 5-inch circles about ⅜ inch thick.

7. Place the circles on the ungreased cookie sheets. Using the tines of a fork, press a 1-inch border design about ⅛ inch deep around the edges. Prick the dough all over with the fork. Then with a sharp knife score the dough into 8 equal wedges; do not cut completely through.

8. Bake for 20 minutes. Remove the shortbread from the oven and cut into wedges, following the scored marks. Return the cookies to the oven for 3 to 5 minutes, or until they turn a pale golden brown around the edges. Cool on racks.

SHORTBREAD TIPS

Like pastry, shortbread should be handled as little and as lightly as possible since handling the dough too much will toughen it.

Traditionally served on New Year's Eve, Scottish shortbread was baked in the shape of a large disk with notched edges to symbolize the Celtic sun god. Today, carved molds are sometimes used to pattern shortbread, but plain circles and hand-crimped edges are more usual.

ENGLISH GINGERSNAPS

Makes 35 to 40 cookies

2 cups all-purpose flour
1 ½ teaspoons baking soda
½ teaspoon salt
1 teaspoon ground cinnamon
1 ½ teaspoons ground ginger
½ teaspoon ground cloves
⅛ teaspoon grated nutmeg
6 ounces (1 ½ sticks) butter
1 cup packed light brown sugar
1 egg, lightly beaten
¼ cup dark molasses
⅓ cup granulated sugar

1. Preheat the oven to 375° F. Butter cookie sheets.

2. Sift together the flour, baking soda, salt, cinnamon, ginger, cloves and nutmeg.

3. Cream the butter and brown sugar until smooth and light.

4. Beat in the egg and then the molasses.

5. Stir in the dry ingredients until thoroughly incorporated.

6. Pinch off pieces of dough and shape into 1-inch balls. Roll each ball in granulated sugar to cover completely and place them 2 ½ inches apart on the buttered cookie sheets. Bake the cookies for 15 minutes, or until almost firm to the touch. Cool on racks.

VANILLA SNAPS

Makes 35 to 40 cookies

4 ounces (1 stick) butter
1 cup granulated sugar
1 egg, lightly beaten
¼ cup light corn syrup
1 teaspoon vanilla extract
2 cups all-purpose flour
½ teaspoon baking soda
½ teaspoon salt
flavored sugar for coating (see page 16)

1. Preheat the oven to 350° F. Butter cookie sheets.

2. Cream the butter and sugar until light and fluffy. Add the egg, corn syrup and vanilla extract; blend well.

3. Mix the flour, baking soda and salt together; add to the creamed mixture and combine thoroughly. Chill the dough for 30 minutes.

4. Pinch off pieces of dough, shape into 1-inch balls and roll in the flavored sugar, covering each ball completely. Place the balls 3 inches apart on the buttered cookie sheets. With the bottom of a glass, flatten the cookies to approximately ¼-inch thickness. Bake for 10 to 12 minutes, or until the cookies are firm. Transfer the cookies to racks to cool completely.

CHOCOLATE SNAPS. In a heavy saucepan over low heat, or in the top pan of a double boiler, melt 4 squares (4 ounces) unsweetened baking chocolate. Cool to room temperature. Substitute dark corn syrup for light in step 2. Add the chocolate to the creamed mixture at the end of step 2. Roll the balls in vanilla sugar (see page 16).

ORANGE SNAPS. In place of vanilla extract, add 3 tablespoons fresh orange juice, 2 teaspoons freshly grated orange zest or, if fresh orange zest is unavailable, 2 tablespoons prepared orange zest (see page 15) at the end of step 2. Increase flour to 2¼ cups. Roll the balls in orange sugar.

LEMON SNAPS. Omit vanilla extract; add 2 teaspoons freshly grated lemon zest or 2 tablespoons prepared lemon zest (see page 15) and 3 tablespoons fresh lemon juice at the end of step 2. Increase flour to 2¼ cups. Roll the balls in lemon sugar.

VANILLA NUT SNAPS. Increase vanilla extract to 2 teaspoons. Stir in 1 cup finely chopped pecans at the end of step 3. Roll the balls in vanilla sugar (see page 16).

CINNAMON SNAPS. Add 2 teaspoons ground cinnamon into the dry ingredients in step 3. Roll the balls in cinnamon sugar (see page 16).

PFEFFERNUESSE

These cookies improve with age. To keep them fresh and soft, place a slice of apple in the container.

Makes 45 to 50 cookies

1½ cups all-purpose flour
1 teaspoon ground cinnamon
½ teaspoon grated nutmeg
¼ teaspoon ground cloves
¼ teaspoon white pepper
⅛ teaspoon ground ginger
¼ teaspoon salt
2 eggs, lightly beaten
1 cup granulated sugar
¼ cup ground blanched almonds
2 tablespoons chopped candied green cherries
2 tablespoons chopped candied red cherries
1 teaspoon each of grated lemon and orange zest
¼ cup rum
2 cups confectioners' sugar

PFEFFERNUESSE

These spicy, orange-rind-flavored cookies are traditional German Christmas cookies. Hand-shaped into small sugar-coated or glazed balls, they are an essential part of the holiday in Bavaria.

1. Preheat the oven to 350° F. 15 to 30 minutes before you are ready to bake the cookies. Butter cookie sheets.

2. Sift together the flour, cinnamon, nutmeg, cloves, white pepper, ginger and salt.

3. Beat the eggs and granulated sugar together until thick and pale yellow. Stir in the ground almonds, green and red candied cherries, orange and lemon zest. Stir in the dry ingredients and combine thoroughly. Chill the dough for 8 hours or overnight.

4. Roll the dough into 1-inch balls and place them 1 inch apart on the buttered cookie sheets. Bake for 15 minutes, or until cookies are firm and lightly browned. Cool slightly on racks.

5. While still warm, use a pastry brush to coat each cookie with approximately ¼ teaspoon rum. Roll the cookies in the confectioners' sugar. Store in airtight tins for 2 or 3 days before serving.

GLAZED PFEFFERNUESSE. Mix together 1½ cups sifted confectioners' sugar with 3 tablespoons milk. Blend well. After the cookies have cooled completely, dip them into the glaze. Place on wax paper to dry. Store in an airtight tin for 2 or 3 days before serving.

SPRINGERLE

This is a traditional German Christmas cookie flavored with aniseed and lemon and rolled and cut with a springerle rolling pin or pressed into molds. These cookies should be allowed to mellow in a tightly covered container for several weeks before serving.

Makes 45 to 50 cookies

4 eggs
2 cups granulated sugar
2 teaspoons lemon zest
4⅓ cups flour
1 teaspoon baking powder
½ teaspoon salt
2 teaspoons aniseeds

1. Preheat the oven to 300° F. 15 to 30 minutes before you are ready to bake the cookies. Butter cookie sheets.

2. Beat the eggs until foamy. Gradually add the sugar and continue to beat for about 5 minutes, or until the mixture is pale yellow and forms a ribbon. Beat in the lemon zest.

3. Gradually add the flour, baking powder and salt; beat just until combined.

4. Turn the dough out on a lightly floured board and knead it until smooth and pliable. Roll it into a rectangular shape about ¼ inch thick and slightly wider than a springerle rolling pin. Place the rolling pin firmly on the dough and press and roll the pin along the dough.

5. Sprinkle the buttered cookie sheet with the aniseeds. Cut the cookies with a sharp knife, separate them, and transfer to the cookie sheet, placing them about 1 inch apart. Allow the cookies to dry for 12 hours.

6. Bake the cookies for 15 to 18 minutes, or until they are lightly golden on the bottoms. Cool on racks. Store in an airtight container for 1 to 2 weeks before serving.

ICEBOX COOKIES

Icebox Cookies lend themselves to endless variations. The log-shaped dough can be frozen for up to 6 months.

Makes 25 to 30 cookies

4 ounces (1 stick) butter
½ cup granulated sugar
1 egg, lightly beaten
½ teaspoon vanilla extract
1½ cups flour
½ teaspoon baking powder
½ teaspoon salt
flavoring (lemon, chocolate, cinnamon nut or date filling)

1. Preheat the oven to 375° F. 15 to 30 minutes before you are ready to bake the cookies. Butter cookie sheets.

2. Cream the butter and sugar until light and fluffy. Blend in the egg; stir in the vanilla extract.

3. Sift the flour, baking powder and salt together. Stir into the creamed mixture until thoroughly incorporated.

4. Chill the dough for 1 hour, or until it can be easily shaped into 2 logs about 1½ inches wide and 5½ inches long. Freeze the logs for at least 1 hour, or until firm.

5. When ready to bake, cut the logs into ⅜-inch-thick slices, and place them 1 inch apart on the buttered cookie sheets. Bake for 8 to 10 minutes, or until lightly browned around the edges. Cool on racks.

ICEBOX LEMON COOKIES. Add 2 teaspoons lemon zest and 1 tablespoon lemon juice at the end of step 2. After the dough has chilled, form into logs and roll in ½ cup lemon sugar (see page 16), pressing firmly so that the sugar sticks to the dough. When ready to bake, continue as directed in step 5.

ICEBOX PINWHEEL COOKIES. Substitute light brown sugar for granulated and use 1 egg yolk instead of the whole egg. In a heavy saucepan over low heat, or in the top pan of a double boiler, melt 1 square (1 ounce) of unsweetened chocolate. Cool the chocolate to room temperature. At the end of step 3, divide the dough into halves; add the chocolate to one half. When ready to shape the dough, roll out each portion of the dough on a lightly floured surface or between 2 sheets of wax paper. Place the chocolate dough over the plain and roll into a tight log starting at longer side; wrap and freeze. When ready to bake, continue as directed in step 5.

ICEBOX CINNAMON NUT COOKIES. Chill the dough for at least 1 hour. Combine 1 cup finely chopped walnuts, 2 teaspoons ground cinnamon, 2 tablespoons honey and 2 tablespoons butter in a small saucepan. Over low heat, stir the mixture until the butter melts and the nuts are evenly coated. Cool to room temperature. Roll the chilled dough into a rectangle about ⅜ inch thick. Spread evenly with the cinnamon and nut mixture; starting at the longer side, roll into a log. Wrap and freeze. When ready to bake, continue as directed in step 5.

ICEBOX DATE-FILLED COOKIES. Chill the dough for at least 1 hour. To prepare the date filling, combine ½ cup chopped pitted dates, ¼ cup sugar, 1 tablespoon butter and ½ cup water in a saucepan. Bring the mixture to a boil over moderate heat and continue to cook for 5 to 7 minutes, or until the mixture thickens. Cool completely. Roll the chilled dough into a rectangle about ⅜ inch thick. Spread the date mixture over the dough; starting at the longer side, roll into a log. Wrap and freeze. When ready to bake, continue as directed in step 5.

SPRITZ COOKIES

Makes 30 to 35 cookies

8 ounces (2 sticks) butter
⅔ cup granulated sugar
1 egg
1 teaspoon vanilla extract
¼ teaspoon grated lemon zest
2¼ cups flour
¼ teaspoon salt
colored sugar for decoration (see page 16)

1. Preheat the oven to 375° F.

2. Cream the butter and sugar until light and fluffy; beat in the egg. Stir in the vanilla and lemon zest, blending well.

3. Sift the flour and salt together; gradually stir into the creamed mixture, making a soft dough.

4. Force the dough out of a cookie press fitted with a decorative blade onto the ungreased cookie sheets, leaving 1½ inches between the cookies. Sprinkle with colored sugar (optional).

5. Bake for 10 to 12 minutes, or until lightly browned around the edges. Cool on racks.

SPECULAAS

This much-loved Dutch Christmas spice cookie is traditionally shaped in a carved wooden mold. The cookies take their name from the method of molding the dough—*speculaas* has its source in *speculum*, the Latin word for mirror.

Makes 45 to 50 cookies

2½ cups all-purpose flour
¼ teaspoon salt
2 teaspoons ground cinnamon
1 teaspoon ground cloves
1 teaspoon grated nutmeg
¼ teaspoon ground cardamom
¼ teaspoon ground ginger
6 ounces (1½ sticks) butter
1 cup packed light brown sugar
1 egg
½ cup sliced almonds
½ cup crystal sugar for decoration
½ cup slivered blanched almonds for decoration

1. Preheat the oven to 350° F. Butter cookie sheets.

2. Sift the flour, salt, cinnamon, cloves, nutmeg, cardamom and ginger together.

3. Cream the butter and sugar together until smooth and light. Beat in the egg; stir in the dry ingredients until thoroughly combined. Mix in the sliced almonds. Gather the dough into a ball and divide into quarters.

4. On a surface lightly dusted with flour, press the dough into rectangles, using the palm of your hand. Using as little flour as possible, roll out the dough to about ⅛-inch thickness. Repeat with the remaining dough.

5. Using a sharp knife, even the edges. Cut the dough into approximately 2- x 3-inch rectangles. Sprinkle generously with crystal sugar and press on the slivered almonds; transfer to the buttered cookie sheets.

6. Bake the cookies for 10 to 12 minutes, or until the edges start to brown and cookies feel firm to the touch. Cool on racks.

ORNAMENT COOKIES

Christmas trees in the nineteenth century were abundantly decorated with hanging cookies of this type. These cookies are as edible as they are beautiful.

Makes 45 to 50 cookies

6 ounces (1½ sticks) butter
1¼ cups granulated sugar
3 eggs, lightly beaten
1 teaspoon vanilla extract
3½ cups all-purpose flour
½ teaspoon salt
½ teaspoon grated nutmeg
¼ cup brandy

1. Preheat the oven to 375° F. Butter cookie sheets.

2. Cream the butter and sugar together until light and fluffy.

3. Blend in the eggs until well combined; stir in the vanilla extract.

4. Sift together the flour, salt and nutmeg. Mix half of the dry ingredients into the creamed mixture. Stir in the brandy and mix in remaining dry ingredients until thoroughly incorporated.

5. Chill the dough for 4 to 6 hours, or until firm.

6. Divide the dough into 4 portions; keep each portion refrigerated until needed. On a floured surface roll the dough to ⅜-inch thickness. Cut out shapes with 2½- to 3-inch fancy cookie cutters (i.e., Christmas trees, stars, wreaths, hearts, etc.). Transfer the cookies to the buttered cookie sheets. Using a toothpick, make a hole at the top of each cookie.

7. Bake the cookies for 10 to 12 minutes, or until they start to brown along the edges. Transfer to racks to cool.

8. Insert a ribbon or piece of kitchen string through the hole—and hang the cookies as directed.

ALMOND TUILES

These crisp, curved wafer cookies are named after the red brick roof tiles typically found atop Mediterranean villas. When these cookies are first removed from the oven, they can be shaped; as they cool, they become brittle and retain that shape.

Makes 20 to 25 cookies

3 ounces (¾ stick) butter
½ cup granulated sugar
¼ teaspoon vanilla extract
½ cup all-purpose flour
pinch of salt
4 egg whites, lightly beaten
1 cup sliced blanched almonds

1. Preheat the oven to 375° F. Generously butter cookie sheets.

2. Cream the butter; gradually add the sugar, beating until thoroughly combined. Stir in the vanilla extract.

3. Mix the flour and salt together and mix into the creamed mixture. Fold in the egg whites and blend well. Stir in the sliced almonds.

4. Drop the batter by level tablespoons 5 inches apart onto the buttered cookie sheets. Spread the dough with the back of a teaspoon to make 3-inch circles and evenly distribute the almonds with the tines of a fork that has been dipped into water. If the batter sticks, wet the fork again. Bake only a few cookies at a time as they must be shaped immediately after being removed from the oven.

5. Bake for 6 to 8 minutes, or until the cookies have spread but are still white. Remove them from the oven for 1 minute to allow the excess moisture to evaporate. Return the cookies to the oven and bake for 2 to 4 minutes more, or until the cookies are golden brown around the edges and lightly browned in the centers.

6. With a thin metal spatula remove the cookies and immediately place them on a rolling pin to shape. Press each cookie into a tile shape; remove to racks to cool, curved side up. If the wafers harden before you can shape them all, return the cookie sheet to the oven and warm the cookies until they are malleable again. It is always easier for handling to bake only 6 cookies at a time.

CHOCOLATE HAZELNUT TUILES. Add 1 tablespoon Dutch-process cocoa powder in step 3. In place of sliced almonds, use ½ cup finely chopped blanched hazelnuts.

LEMON TUILES. In place of vanilla extract, use 1 teaspoon fresh lemon juice and 2 teaspoons grated lemon zest.

CIGARETTES. Instead of shaping the cookies over a rolling pin, remove 1 cookie at a time and immediately roll it around the thin handle of a wooden spoon. Place on racks to cool.

CINNAMON STICKS. In place of vanilla extract, add 1 ½ teaspoons ground cinnamon and a pinch of grated nutmeg. Add cinnamon sugar for a garnish. Instead of shaping the cookies over a rolling pin, remove 1 cookie at a time and immediately roll it around the thin handle of a wooden spoon. Place on a rack to cool and sprinkle with cinnamon sugar.

ALMOND MACAROONS

Makes 18 to 20 cookies

1 cup almond paste
1 cup granulated sugar
2 egg whites
⅓ cup pine nuts

1. Preheat the oven to 325° F. Generously butter cookie sheets.

2. Break the almond paste into small pieces.

3. Add the sugar and egg whites and, using your hands, work the mixture into a smooth paste. Let the dough stand at room temperature for 1 hour.

4. Form the dough into 1-inch balls and place them 2 ½ inches apart on the buttered cookie sheets. Press pine nuts onto the top of each cookie.

5. Bake for 20 minutes, or until golden around the edges. Cool on racks.

MADELEINES

Madeleines are best served the day they are baked; however, they can be kept in an air-tight, container in the freezer.

Makes 60 to 65 cookies

5½ tablespoons butter
2 eggs
½ cup granulated sugar
1 teaspoon grated lemon zest
½ teaspoon vanilla extract
½ cup all-purpose flour
¼ teaspoon salt
sugar for sprinkling

1. Preheat the oven to 350° F. Butter and flour madeleine molds.

2. In the top pan of a double boiler, or in a small heavy saucepan over low heat, melt the butter. Skim off the foam; cool completely. Pour the butter into a small bowl, leaving the milky residue in the pan.

3. Beat the eggs until foamy. Gradually add the sugar and continue to beat the mixture for about 10 minutes, or until it has tripled in volume. Beat in the zest and vanilla extract.

4. Sift the flour and salt together. Divide the flour mixture into 3 equal parts. Sift one portion of the mixture over the batter. Gently but thoroughly fold the sifted mixture into the batter until incorporated. Repeat with each of the remaining portions.

5. Pour the melted butter around the edge of the batter and quickly but gently fold the butter into the batter until absorbed.

6. Spoon the batter into the prepared molds to two thirds full. Bake the cookies for 8 to 10 minutes, or until they are golden and spring back when pressed with your finger. Transfer the mold to a rack. Press each madeleine with your finger on the shallow side to release them from the molds. Sprinkle with sugar while still warm. Cool completely.

CHOCOLATE MADELEINES. Omit lemon zest. In step 4, add ¼ cup Dutch-process cocoa to the flour.

"She sent for one of these short, plump little cakes called 'petites madeleines,' which look as though they had been molded in the fluted scallop of the pilgrim's shell. And soon, mechanically, weary after a dull day with the prospect of a depressing morrow, I raised to my lips a spoonful of the cake...a shudder ran through my whole body and I stopped, intent upon the extraordinary changes that were taking place."

MARCEL PROUST
Remembrance of Things Past

LADYFINGERS

Makes 18 to 20 cookies

3 eggs, separated
⅛ teaspoon salt
½ cup granulated sugar
½ teaspoon vanilla extract
⅔ cup all-purpose flour
½ cup confectioners' sugar for coating

1. Preheat the oven to 350° F. Line cookie sheets with parchment paper.

2. Beat the egg whites until foamy. Add salt; continue beating. Gradually add the granulated sugar and continue beating until the mixture is shiny and stiff peaks form.

3. Beat the egg yolks until thick and pale yellow in color; mix in the vanilla extract just until blended. Fold the yolk mixture into the beaten egg whites.

4. Sift the flour. Divide into 2 equal portions. Sift one portion of the mixture over the egg mixture. Gently but thoroughly fold the sifted mixture into the batter until incorporated. Repeat with the remaining portion.

5. Using a pastry bag fitted with a number 8 plain tube, pipe out 1- x 4-inch finger shapes on the lined cookie sheets. Sift confectioners' sugar over the tops. Bake for 15 minutes, or until lightly golden on top. Cool on racks. Peel the ladyfingers off the paper.

SPONGE PENNIES. Instead of finger shapes, pipe out circles, leaving 1½ inches between the cookies. Bake for 8 to 10 minutes, or until golden on top.

MERINGUE KISSES

Makes 20 to 25 cookies

3 egg whites
⅛ teaspoon salt
½ cup granulated sugar
1 teaspoon rum extract

1. Preheat the oven to 250° F. Line cookie sheets with parchment paper.

2. Beat the egg whites until foamy. Add the salt and continue beating until soft peaks form. Gradually add the sugar and continue to beat until the whites form stiff peaks and the mixture is shiny. Mix in the rum extract.

3. Using a number 4 star tube, pipe out kisses, placing the cookies 1 inch apart. Bake the cookies for 40 minutes, or until they are dry and barely have a hint of color. Turn off the oven and leave the cookies in it to dry out for 3 hours. Peel off the parchment paper.

CHOCOLATE FLECKED MERINGUES.
Add 1 ounce of grated semisweet chocolate to the meringue mixture at the end of step 2.

COCOA KISSES. Sift ¼ cup Dutch-process cocoa onto the meringue mixture at end of step 2 and fold in.

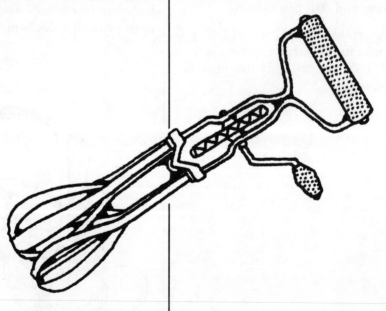

SUGAR CONES

These lovely cone-shaped cookies can be filled with fluffy whipped cream or served with a dish of ice cream.

Makes 30 to 35 cookies

⅔ cup all-purpose flour
⅛ teaspoon salt
⅛ teaspoon baking soda
¼ teaspoon ground cinnamon
$1/16$ teaspoon grated nutmeg
⅓ cup packed light brown sugar
5½ tablespoons butter, chilled
1½ tablespoons dark corn syrup

1. Preheat the oven to 375° F. Butter cookie sheets.

2. Combine the flour, salt, baking soda, cinnamon, nutmeg and brown sugar.

3. Cut the butter into the flour mixture with 2 knives or a pastry blender until the mixture resembles coarse oatmeal. Stir in the corn syrup until well blended. Chill the mixture for 2 hours, or until firm.

4. Form the dough into 3¼-inch balls. Place them 5 inches apart on the buttered cookie sheets. Press each cookie flat with the bottom of a glass that has been buttered and then dipped in sugar. Dip the glass into sugar again for each cookie cone.

5. Bake for 10 minutes, or until dark brown. Cool the cookies on the sheets for about 1 minute before removing them one at a time—with a wide metal spatula. Shape into cones by wrapping the semisoft cookies immediately around a horn mold or your finger. Place on racks to cool completely.

CHOCOLATE DIPPED SUGAR CONES.

In a heavy saucepan over low heat, or in the top pan of a double boiler, melt 6 squares (6 ounces) semisweet chocolate. Cool slightly. When the cones have cooled completely, dip them about 1 inch deep into the chocolate. Allow the excess chocolate to drip back into the saucepan. Place on wax paper and allow the chocolate to harden.

ITALIAN ALMOND MACAROONS

Makes 18 to 20 cookies

2 egg whites
½ cup granulated sugar
1 tablespoon Amaretto liqueur
¾ cup ground unblanched almonds

1. Preheat the oven to 325° F. Line cookie sheets with parchment paper.

2. Beat the egg whites until soft peaks form. Gradually add the sugar. Continue to beat the whites until they are stiff and glossy.

3. Mix in the Amaretto, 1 teaspoon at a time. Sprinkle the ground almonds over the mixture and gently but thoroughly combine.

4. Using a tablespoon or pastry bag fitted with a number 4 plain tube, pipe out the mixture 2 inches apart onto the lined cookie sheets. Bake for 25 to 30 minutes, or until firm and dry.

5. With the cookies still on the parchment, place on racks; cool slightly. Peel off the paper and return the macaroons to racks to cool.

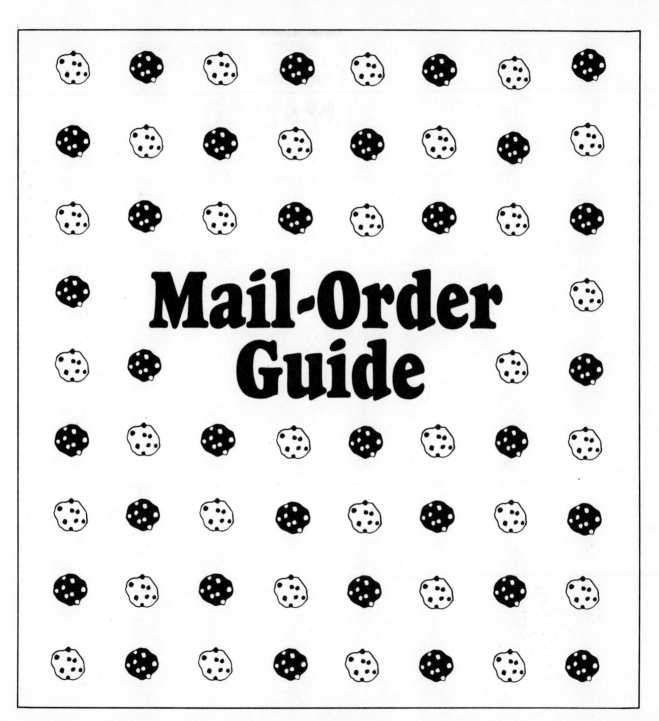

Mail-Order Guide

Bazaar Français of the Market, Inc.
668 Sixth Ave.
New York, NY 10010
Equipment, excellent selection

Bissinger's
205 West 4th St.
Cincinnati, OH 45202
Equipment and selection of chocolate

Bridge Kitchenware
214 East 52nd St.
New York, NY 10022
Equipment

Dean & DeLuca, Inc.
121 Prince St.
New York, NY 10012
Spices, equipment, exotic ingredients, Medjool dates

Istanbul Express
2432 Durant Ave.
Berkeley, CA 94704
Excellent selection of chocolate

The Kobos Company
5531 S.W. Macadam
Portland, OR 97201
Equipment, spices, minimuffin tins, tartlet pans

Lekvar by the Barrel
H. Roth and Son
1577 First Ave.
New York, NY 10028
Excellent selection of equipment and ingredients, vanilla beans, candied fruit, spices (whole or ground), sugar crystals

Maid of Scandinavia
3244 Raleigh Ave.
Minneapolis, MN 55416
Equipment and ingredients, including chocolate, vanilla beans and spices

Paprikas Weiss Importer
1546 Second Ave.
New York, NY 10028
Ingredients, including vanilla beans, spices (whole and ground) and some equipment

Williams-Sonoma
Mail-Order Department
P.O. Box 7456
San Francisco, CA 94120
Excellent selection of equipment and some ingredients, books, molds, cookie cutters

Zabar's
2245 Broadway
New York, NY 10024
Discount equipment and most ingredients

Index